I0017966

Arduino plays with Angry Bird Game Controller, Fingerprint Based Biometric, Brilliant Knock Detecting Door etc... (Best Projects)

Copyright © Anbazhagan.k
All rights reserved 2019.

Arduino plays with Angry Bird Game Controller, Fingerprint Based Biometric , Brilliant Knock Detecting Door etc.. Projects

CONTENTS

Function

ACKNOWLEDGMENTS

The writer might want to recognize the diligent work of the article group in assembling this book. He might likewise want to recognize the diligent work of the Raspberry Pi Foundation and the Arduino bunch for assembling items and networks that help to make the Internet of Things increasingly open to the overall population. Yahoo for the democratization of innovation!

INTRODUCTION

The Internet of Things (IOT) is a perplexing idea comprised of numerous PCs and numerous correspondence ways. Some IOT gadgets are associated with the Internet and some are most certainly not. Some IOT gadgets structure swarms that convey among themselves. Some are intended for a solitary reason, while some are increasingly universally useful PCs. This book is intended to demonstrate to you the IOT from the back to front. By structure IOT gadgets, the per user will comprehend the essential ideas and will almost certainly develop utilizing the rudiments to make his or her very own IOT applications. These included ventures will tell the per user the best way to assemble their very own IOT ventures and to develop the models appeared. The significance of Computer Security in IOT gadgets is additionally talked about and different systems for protecting the IOT from unapproved clients or programmers. The most significant takeaway from this book is in structure the tasks yourself.

1.FINGERPRINT BASED BIOMETRIC ATTENDANCE SYSTEM UTILIZING ARDUINO

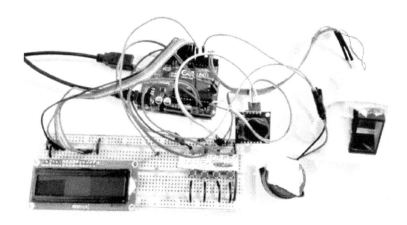

Participation frameworks are regularly utilized frameworks to check the nearness in workplaces and schools. From physically denoting the participation in participation registers to utilizing cutting edge applications and biometric frameworks, these frameworks have improved essentially. We have secured two of other electronic participation framework ventures in our past using RFID as well as AVR microcontroller, 8051 as well as raspberry Pi. In this task, we utilized unique finger impression Module as well as Arduino to take as well as keep participation information as well as records. By using rare finger impression sensor, the framework will turn out to be increasingly secure for the clients. Following areas clarifies specialized subtleties of making a unique mark based biometric participation framework utilizing Arduino.

Required Components

- Arduino -1
- Finger print module -1
- Push Button   - 4
- LEDs -1
- 1K Resistor -2
- 2.2K resistor -1
- Power
- Connecting wires
- Box
- Buzzer -1
- 16x2 LCD -1
- Bread Board -1
- RTC Module -1

Project Description:

In this unique finger impression participation framework circuit, we utilized Fingerprint Sensor module to verify a genuine individual or representative by taking their finger contribution to the framework. Here we are utilizing 4 push catches to enlist, Delete, UP/Down. Enlist and DEL key has triple highlights. Enlist key is utilized for enlistment of another individual into the framework. So when the client needs to select new finger then he/she have to press ENROLL key then LCD requests the ID, where client need to be store the unique mark picture. Presently on the off chance that right now client wouldn't like to continue further, at that point he/she can press ENROLL key again to return. This time ENROLL key carry on as Back key, for example Enlist key has both enlistment and back capacity. Other than select key is additionally used to download participation information over sequential screen. Essentially, DEL/OK key additionally has a similar twofold capacity like when client enlists new finger, at that point he/she have to choose finger ID by utilizing another two key to be specific UP and DOWN. Presently client need to press DEL/OK key (this time this key carry on like OK) to continue with chosen ID. Del key is used to reset or erase information from EEPROM of Arduino.

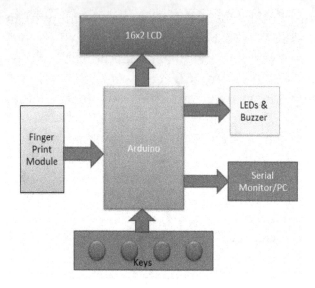

FingerPrint module:

Unique mark sensor module catches unique mark picture and after that changes over it into the proportional layout and spares them into its memory according to chosen ID by Arduino. All the procedure is directed by Arduino like taking a picture of unique mark, convert it into layouts and putting away as ID and so forth. You can check some more ventures utilizing unique finger impression module:

Unique mark based security framework

Unique mark based biometric casting a ballot machine

Here we have included a Yellow LED which demonstrates that unique mark module is prepared to take a picture of the finger. A ringer is likewise utilized for different signs. Arduino is the principle part of this framework it is liable for control of the entire framework.

Working of Fingerprint Based Attendance System

Working of this unique mark participation framework venture is genuinely basic. As a matter of first importance, the client needs to select fingerprints of the client with the assistance of push catches. To do this, client need to press ENROLL key and after that LCD requests entering ID for the unique mark to spare it in memory by ID name. So now client needs to enter ID by spending/DOWN keys. Subsequent to choosing ID, client needs to squeeze OK key (DEL key). Presently LCD will request to place finger over the unique mark module. Presently client needs to put his finger over unique mark module and after that the module takes finger picture. Presently the LCD will say to expel finger from unique mark module, as well as again request to place finger once more. Presently client needs to put his finger again and module takes a picture and convert it into layouts and stores it by chose ID into the unique mark module's memory. Presently the client will be enlisted and he/she can encourage participation by putting their finger over unique mark module. By a similar technique, every one of the clients will be enrolled into the framework.

Presently if the client have to evacuate or erase any of the put away ID or rare mark, at that point he/she have to press DEL key. Once erase key is squeezed LCD will request to choose ID that should be erased. Presently client have to choose ID as well as press OK key (same DEL key). Presently LCD will tell you that unique mark has been erased effectively.

How Attendance functions in this Fingerprint Attendance System Project:

At whatever point client place his finger over unique finger impression module at that point unique finger impression module catches finger picture, and search if any ID is related with this finger impression in the framework. On the off chance that unique finger impression ID is distinguished, at that point LCD will show Attendance enrolled and in a similar time ringer will blare once and LED will mood killer until the framework is prepared to take input once more.

Alongside the unique mark module, we have likewise utilized a RTC module for Time and date. Time and date are running constantly in the framework. So Arduino require significant investment and date at whatever point a genuine client puts his finger over unique finger impression and spare them in the EEPROM at the assigned opening of memory.

Here we have made 5 client space in this framework for 30 days. By squeezing the RESET catch in Arduino and afterward promptly select key will be liable for downloading participation information over sequential screen from the Arduino EEPROM Memory.

Memory Management:

We have 1023 byte memory in Arduino UNO out of which we have 1018 byte to store information as well as we have taken 5 client participation information for 30 days. What's more, every participation will record time and date so this ends up 7-byte information.

So absolute memory required is

5*30*7=1050 so here we need progressively 32 bytes

Be that as it may, in the event that we will utilize 4 clients, at that point we required

4*30*7=840

Here we have done this task exhibition by taking 5 clients memory. By this, we won't ready to store 32 byte or 5 participation records of the fifth client.

You may attempt it by 4 clients by changing a few lines in code. I have made the remarks in the code where the progressions are required.

Circuit Diagram and Description for Fingerprint Attendance System Project

The circuit of this unique mark based participation framework venture, as appeared in the above chart is very straightforward. It has Arduino for controlling all the procedure of the venture, push button for enlisting, erasing, choosing IDs and for participation, a signal for cautioning, LEDs for sign and LCD to teach client and demonstrating the resultant messages.

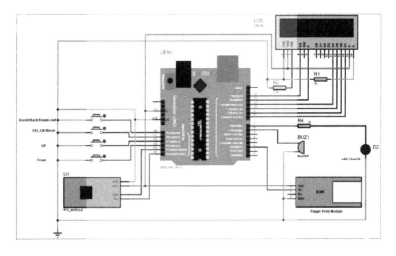

As appeared in the circuit chart, a push catch is legitimately associated with stick A0(ENROL), A1(DEL), A2(UP), A3(DOWN) of Arduino as for the ground And Yellow LED is associated at Digital stick D7 of Arduino concerning ground through a 1k resistor. Unique mark module's Rx and Tx straightforwardly associated at Serial stick D2 and D3 (Software Serial) of Arduino. 5v supply is utilized for driving unique finger impression module taken from Arduino board. A signal is additionally associated at stick A5. A 16x2 LCD is designed in 4-piece mode and its RS, EN, D4, D5, D6, and D7 are legitimately associated at Digital stick D13, D12, D11, D10,D9, and D8 of Arduino.

Code Explanation:

The unique finger impression participation framework code for arduino is given in the consequent segments. Despite the fact that the code is clarified well

15

with remarks, we are talking about here couple of significant pieces of the code. We utilized unique mark library for interfacing unique mark module with Arduino board.

Above all else, we incorporate the header record and characterizes info and yield stick and characterize the full scale and announced factors. After this, in arrangement work, we provide guidance to characterized stick and start LCD and unique mark module

After it, we need to compose code for downloading participation information.

```
void setup()

{

    delay(1000);

    lcd.begin(16,2);

    Serial.begin(9600);

    pinMode(enroll, INPUT_PULLUP);

    pinMode(up, INPUT_PULLUP);

    pinMode(down, INPUT_PULLUP);
```

```
pinMode(del, INPUT_PULLUP);

pinMode(match, INPUT_PULLUP);

pinMode(buzzer, OUTPUT);

pinMode(indFinger, OUTPUT);

digitalWrite(buzzer, LOW);

if(digitalRead(enroll) == 0)

{

  digitalWrite(buzzer, HIGH);

  delay(500);

  digitalWrite(buzzer, LOW);

  lcd.clear();

  lcd.print("Please wait");

  lcd.setCursor(0,1);

  lcd.print("Downloding Data");
```

After it, we need to compose code for clearing participation information from EEPROM.

```
if(digitalRead(del) == 0)

  {

    lcd.clear();

    lcd.print("Please Wait");

    lcd.setCursor(0,1);

    lcd.print("Reseting.....");

    for(int i=1000;i<1005;i++)

    EEPROM.write(i,0);

    for(int i=0;i<841;i++)

    EEPROM.write(i, 0xff);

    lcd.clear();

    lcd.print("System Reset");

    delay(1000);

  }
```

After it, we start unique mark module, demonstrating welcome message over LCD and furthermore initeiated RTC module.

After it, in circle work, we have perused RTC time and shown it on LCD

```
void loop()

{

    now = rtc.now();

    lcd.setCursor(0,0);

    lcd.print("Time->");

    lcd.print(now.hour(), DEC);

    lcd.print(':');

    lcd.print(now.minute(), DEC);

    lcd.print(':');

    lcd.print(now.second(), DEC);

    lcd.print("  ");
```

```
lcd.setCursor(0,1);

lcd.print("Date->");

lcd.print(now.day(), DEC);

lcd.print('/');

lcd.print(now.month(), DEC);

lcd.print('/');

lcd.print(now.year(), DEC);
```

After it, hanging tight for the unique mark to take information and contrast caught picture ID and put away IDs. On the off chance that amatch happens, at that point continue with subsequent stage. What's more, checking select del keys also

```
int result = getFingerprintIDez();

if(result > 0)

{

        digitalWrite(indFinger, LOW);

        digitalWrite(buzzer, HIGH);
```

```
delay(100);

digitalWrite(buzzer, LOW);

lcd.clear();

lcd.print("ID:");

lcd.print(result);

lcd.setCursor(0,1);

lcd.print("Please Wait....");

delay(1000);

attendance(result);

lcd.clear();

lcd.print("Attendance ");

lcd.setCursor(0,1);

lcd.print("Registed");

delay(1000);

digitalWrite(indFinger, HIGH);
```

```
      return;

}
```

Given void checkKeys() work is utilized for checking Enroll or DEL key is squeezed or not and what to do whenever squeezed. On the off chance that the Enroll key squeezed the Enroll() work is called and DEL key press at that point erase() work is called.

void delet() work is utilized for entering ID to be erased and calling uint8_t deleteFingerprint(uint8_t id) work that will erase finger from records.

Given Function is accustomed to taking unique finger impression picture and convert them into the layout and spare also by chosen ID into the unique finger impression module memory.

```
uint8_t getFingerprintEnroll()

{

  int p = -1;

  lcd.clear();

  lcd.print("finger ID:");
```

```
lcd.print(id);

lcd.setCursor(0,1);

lcd.print("Place Finger");

delay(2000);

while (p != FINGERPRINT_OK)

{

  p = finger.getImage();

..... .....

....... ....
```

Given capacity is utilized for putting away participation time and date in the apportioned opening of EEPROM

```
void attendance(int id)

{

  int user=0,eepLoc=0;

  if(id == 1)
```

```
{

 eepLoc=0;

 user=user1++;

}

else if(id == 2)

{

 eepLoc=210;

 user=user2++;

}

else if(id == 3)

.... ....

.....
```

Given capacity is accustomed to getting information from EEPROM and send to sequential screen

```
void download(int eepIndex)
```

```
{

        if(EEPROM.read(eepIndex)!= 0xff)

        {

         Serial.print("T->");

         if(EEPROM.read(eepIndex)<10)

         Serial.print('0');

         Serial.print(EEPROM.read(eepIndex++));

         Serial.print(':');

         if(EEPROM.read(eepIndex)<10)

         Serial.print('0');

         Serial.print(EEPROM.read(eepIndex++));

     .... ....

     .....
```

Code

```
#include<EEPROM.h>
#include<LiquidCrystal.h>
LiquidCrystal lcd(13,12,11,10,9,8);
```

```
#include <SoftwareSerial.h>
SoftwareSerial fingerPrint(2, 3);

#include <Wire.h>
#include "RTClib.h"
RTC_DS1307 rtc;

#include "Adafruit_Fingerprint.h"
uint8_t id;
Adafruit_Fingerprint finger = Adafruit_Finger-
print(&fingerPrint);

#define enroll 14
#define del 15
#define up 16
#define down 17
#define match 5
#define indFinger 7
#define buzzer 5

#define records 4  // 5 for 5 user

int user1,user2,user3,user4,user5;

DateTime now;

void setup()
{
  delay(1000);
  lcd.begin(16,2);
  Serial.begin(9600);
  pinMode(enroll, INPUT_PULLUP);
  pinMode(up, INPUT_PULLUP);
  pinMode(down, INPUT_PULLUP);
  pinMode(del, INPUT_PULLUP);
  pinMode(match, INPUT_PULLUP);
```

```
pinMode(buzzer, OUTPUT);
pinMode(indFinger, OUTPUT);
digitalWrite(buzzer, LOW);
if(digitalRead(enroll) == 0)
{
 digitalWrite(buzzer, HIGH);
 delay(500);
 digitalWrite(buzzer, LOW);
 lcd.clear();
 lcd.print("Please wait");
 lcd.setCursor(0,1);
 lcd.print("Downloding Data");
 Serial.println("Please wait");
 Serial.println("Downloding Data..");
 Serial.println();
 Serial.print("S.No.     ");
 for(int i=0;i<records;i++)
 {
    digitalWrite(buzzer, HIGH);
 delay(500);
 digitalWrite(buzzer, LOW);
  Serial.print("    User ID");
  Serial.print(i+1);
  Serial.print("          ");
 }
 Serial.println();
 int eepIndex=0;
 for(int i=0;i<30;i++)
 {
  if(i+1<10)
```

```
  Serial.print('0');
  Serial.print(i+1);
  Serial.print("      ");
  eepIndex=(i*7);
  download(eepIndex);
  eepIndex=(i*7)+210;
  download(eepIndex);
  eepIndex=(i*7)+420;
  download(eepIndex);
  eepIndex=(i*7)+630;
  download(eepIndex);
 // eepIndex=(i*7)+840;  // 5th user
 // download(eepIndex);
  Serial.println();
 }
}
if(digitalRead(del)==0)
{
 lcd.clear();
 lcd.print("Please Wait");
 lcd.setCursor(0,1);
 lcd.print("Reseting.....");
 for(int i=1000;i<1005;i++)
 EEPROM.write(i,0);
 for(int i=0;i<841;i++)
 EEPROM.write(i, 0xff);
 lcd.clear();
 lcd.print("System Reset");
 delay(1000);
 }
```

```
lcd.clear();
lcd.print(" Attendance ");
lcd.setCursor(0,1);
lcd.print("  System  ");
delay(2000);
lcd.clear();
lcd.print("Hello World");
lcd.setCursor(0,1);
lcd.print("Saddam Khan");
delay(2000);
  digitalWrite(buzzer, HIGH);
 delay(500);
 digitalWrite(buzzer, LOW);
for(int i=1000;i<1000+records;i++)
{
if(EEPROM.read(i) == 0xff)
  EEPROM.write(i,0);
}
 finger.begin(57600);
 Serial.begin(9600);
 lcd.clear();
 lcd.print("Finding Module");
 lcd.setCursor(0,1);
 delay(1000);
 if(finger.verifyPassword())
 {
  Serial.println("Found fingerprint sensor!");
  lcd.clear();
```

```
  lcd.print("Found Module ");
  delay(1000);
}
else
{
Serial.println("Did not find fingerprint sensor :(");
lcd.clear();
lcd.print("module not Found");
lcd.setCursor(0,1);
lcd.print("Check Connections");
while (1);
}
 if (! rtc.begin())
  Serial.println("Couldn't find RTC");
 // rtc.adjust(DateTime(F(__DATE__), F(__TIME__)));
 if (! rtc.isrunning())
 {
Serial.println("RTC is NOT running!");
 // following line sets the RTC to the date & time this
sketch was compiled
  rtc.adjust(DateTime(F(__DATE__), F(__TIME__)));
 // This line sets the RTC with an explicit date & time,
for example to set
 // January 21, 2014 at 3am you would call:
 // rtc.adjust(DateTime(2014, 1, 21, 3, 0, 0));
 }
lcd.setCursor(0,0);
lcd.print("Press Match to ");
lcd.setCursor(0,1);
lcd.print("Start System");
```

```
delay(2000);
user1=EEPROM.read(1000);
user2=EEPROM.read(1001);
user3=EEPROM.read(1002);
user4=EEPROM.read(1003);
user5=EEPROM.read(1004);
lcd.clear();
digitalWrite(indFinger, HIGH);


}
void loop()
{
  now = rtc.now();
  lcd.setCursor(0,0);
  lcd.print("Time->");
  lcd.print(now.hour(), DEC);
  lcd.print(':');
  lcd.print(now.minute(), DEC);
  lcd.print(':');
  lcd.print(now.second(), DEC);
  lcd.print("  ");
  lcd.setCursor(0,1);
  lcd.print("Date->");
  lcd.print(now.day(), DEC);
  lcd.print('/');
  lcd.print(now.month(), DEC);
  lcd.print('/');
  lcd.print(now.year(), DEC);
  lcd.print("  ");
```

```
delay(500);
int result=getFingerprintIDez();
if(result>0)
{
    digitalWrite(indFinger, LOW);
    digitalWrite(buzzer, HIGH);
    delay(100);
    digitalWrite(buzzer, LOW);
    lcd.clear();
    lcd.print("ID:");
    lcd.print(result);
    lcd.setCursor(0,1);
    lcd.print("Please Wait....");
    delay(1000);
    attendance(result);
    lcd.clear();
    lcd.print("Attendance ");
    lcd.setCursor(0,1);
    lcd.print("Registed");
    delay(1000);
  digitalWrite(indFinger, HIGH);
  return;
}
checkKeys();
delay(300);
}
//  dmyyhms - 7 bytes
void attendance(int id)
{
 int user=0,eepLoc=0;
```

```
if(id == 1)
{
 eepLoc=0;
 user=user1++;
}
else if(id == 2)
{
 eepLoc=210;
 user=user2++;
}
else if(id == 3)
{
 eepLoc=420;
 user=user3++;
}
else if(id == 4)
{
 eepLoc=630;
 user=user4++;
}
/*else if(id == 5)  // fifth user
{
 eepLoc=840;
 user=user5++;
}*/
else
return;


  int eepIndex=(user*7)+eepLoc;
 EEPROM.write(eepIndex++, now.hour());
```

```
  EEPROM.write(eepIndex++, now.minute());
  EEPROM.write(eepIndex++, now.second());
  EEPROM.write(eepIndex++, now.day());
  EEPROM.write(eepIndex++, now.month());
  EEPROM.write(eepIndex++, now.year()>>8 );
  EEPROM.write(eepIndex++, now.year());

  EEPROM.write(1000,user1);
  EEPROM.write(1001,user2);
  EEPROM.write(1002,user3);
  EEPROM.write(1003,user4);
 // EEPROM.write(4,user5);  // figth user
}
void checkKeys()
{
 if(digitalRead(enroll) == 0)
 {
 lcd.clear();
 lcd.print("Please Wait");
 delay(1000);
 while(digitalRead(enroll) == 0);
 Enroll();
 }
 else if(digitalRead(del) == 0)
 {
 lcd.clear();
 lcd.print("Please Wait");
 delay(1000);
 delet();
 }
}
```

```
void Enroll()
{
  int count=1;
  lcd.clear();
  lcd.print("Enter Finger ID:");
  while(1)
  {
  lcd.setCursor(0,1);
  lcd.print(count);
  if(digitalRead(up) == 0)
  {
   count++;
   if(count>records)
   count=1;
   delay(500);
  }
  else if(digitalRead(down) == 0)
  {
   count--;
   if(count<1)
   count=records;
   delay(500);
  }
  else if(digitalRead(del) == 0)
  {
    id=count;
    getFingerprintEnroll();
    for(int i=0;i<records;i++)
    {
     if(EEPROM.read(i) != 0xff)
```

```
      {
       EEPROM.write(i, id);
       break;
      }
     }
     return;
  }
   else if(digitalRead(enroll) == 0)
  {
     return;
  }
 }
}
void delet()
{
 int count=1;
 lcd.clear();
 lcd.print("Enter Finger ID");
 while(1)
 {
 lcd.setCursor(0,1);
  lcd.print(count);
  if(digitalRead(up) == 0)
  {
   count++;
   if(count>records)
   count=1;
   delay(500);
  }
   else if(digitalRead(down) == 0)
```

```
 {
  count--;
  if(count<1)
  count=records;
  delay(500);
 }
 else if(digitalRead(del)==0)
 {
   id=count;
   deleteFingerprint(id);
   for(int i=0;i<records;i++)
   {
    if(EEPROM.read(i)==id)
    {
     EEPROM.write(i,0xff);
     break;
    }
   }
   return;
 }
  else if(digitalRead(enroll)==0)
 {
   return;
 }
}
}
uint8_t getFingerprintEnroll()
{
 int p = -1;
 lcd.clear();
```

```
lcd.print("finger ID:");
lcd.print(id);
lcd.setCursor(0,1);
lcd.print("Place Finger");
delay(2000);
while (p != FINGERPRINT_OK)
{
 p = finger.getImage();
 switch (p)
 {
 case FINGERPRINT_OK:
  Serial.println("Image taken");
  lcd.clear();
  lcd.print("Image taken");
  break;
 case FINGERPRINT_NOFINGER:
  Serial.println("No Finger");
  lcd.clear();
  lcd.print("No Finger");
  break;
 case FINGERPRINT_PACKETRECIEVEERR:
  Serial.println("Communication error");
  lcd.clear();
  lcd.print("Comm Error");
  break;
 case FINGERPRINT_IMAGEFAIL:
  Serial.println("Imaging error");
  lcd.clear();
  lcd.print("Imaging Error");
  break;
```

```
 default:
  Serial.println("Unknown error");
  lcd.clear();
  lcd.print("Unknown Error");
  break;
 }
}
// OK success!
p = finger.image2Tz(1);
switch (p) {
 case FINGERPRINT_OK:
  Serial.println("Image converted");
  lcd.clear();
  lcd.print("Image converted");
  break;
 case FINGERPRINT_IMAGEMESS:
  Serial.println("Image too messy");
  lcd.clear();
  lcd.print("Image too messy");
  return p;
 case FINGERPRINT_PACKETRECIEVEERR:
  Serial.println("Communication error");
    lcd.clear();
  lcd.print("Comm Error");
  return p;
 case FINGERPRINT_FEATUREFAIL:
  Serial.println("Could not find fingerprint features");
    lcd.clear();
  lcd.print("Feature Not Found");
  return p;
```

```
 case FINGERPRINT_INVALIDIMAGE:
  Serial.println("Could not find fingerprint features");
       lcd.clear();
  lcd.print("Feature Not Found");
  return p;
 default:
  Serial.println("Unknown error");
       lcd.clear();
  lcd.print("Unknown Error");
  return p;
}
Serial.println("Remove finger");
lcd.clear();
lcd.print("Remove Finger");
delay(2000);
p = 0;
while (p != FINGERPRINT_NOFINGER) {
 p = finger.getImage();
}
Serial.print("ID "); Serial.println(id);
p = -1;
Serial.println("Place same finger again");
 lcd.clear();
  lcd.print("Place Finger");
  lcd.setCursor(0,1);
  lcd.print("  Again");
 while (p != FINGERPRINT_OK) {
 p = finger.getImage();
 switch (p) {
 case FINGERPRINT_OK:
```

```
  Serial.println("Image taken");
  break;
 case FINGERPRINT_NOFINGER:
  Serial.print(".");
  break;
 case FINGERPRINT_PACKETRECIEVEERR:
  Serial.println("Communication error");
  break;
 case FINGERPRINT_IMAGEFAIL:
  Serial.println("Imaging error");
  break;
 default:
  Serial.println("Unknown error");
  return;
 }
}
// OK success!
p = finger.image2Tz(2);
switch (p) {
 case FINGERPRINT_OK:
  Serial.println("Image converted");
  break;
 case FINGERPRINT_IMAGEMESS:
  Serial.println("Image too messy");
  return p;
 case FINGERPRINT_PACKETRECIEVEERR:
  Serial.println("Communication error");
  return p;
 case FINGERPRINT_FEATUREFAIL:
  Serial.println("Could not find fingerprint features");
```

```
  return p;
 case FINGERPRINT_INVALIDIMAGE:
  Serial.println("Could not find fingerprint features");
  return p;
 default:
  Serial.println("Unknown error");
  return p;
}
 // OK converted!
  Serial.print("Creating model for #"); Serial.println(id);
 p = finger.createModel();
 if (p == FINGERPRINT_OK) {
  Serial.println("Prints matched!");
 } else if (p == FINGERPRINT_PACKETRECIEVEERR) {
  Serial.println("Communication error");
  return p;
 } else if (p == FINGERPRINT_ENROLLMISMATCH) {
  Serial.println("Fingerprints did not match");
  return p;
 } else {
  Serial.println("Unknown error");
  return p;
 }
 Serial.print("ID "); Serial.println(id);
 p = finger.storeModel(id);
 if (p == FINGERPRINT_OK) {
  Serial.println("Stored!");
  lcd.clear();
  lcd.print("Stored!");
```

```
 delay(2000);
} else if (p == FINGERPRINT_PACKETRECIEVEERR) {
 Serial.println("Communication error");
 return p;
} else if (p == FINGERPRINT_BADLOCATION) {
 Serial.println("Could not store in that location");
 return p;
} else if (p == FINGERPRINT_FLASHERR) {
 Serial.println("Error writing to flash");
 return p;
}
else {
 Serial.println("Unknown error");
 return p;
}
}
int getFingerprintIDez()
{
 uint8_t p = finger.getImage();
 if (p != FINGERPRINT_OK)
 return -1;
 p = finger.image2Tz();
 if (p != FINGERPRINT_OK)
 return -1;
 p = finger.fingerFastSearch();
 if (p != FINGERPRINT_OK)
 {
 lcd.clear();
 lcd.print("Finger Not Found");
 lcd.setCursor(0,1);
```

```
  lcd.print("Try Later");
  delay(2000);
 return -1;
 }
 // found a match!
 Serial.print("Found ID #");
 Serial.print(finger.fingerID);
 return finger.fingerID;
 }
uint8_t deleteFingerprint(uint8_t id)
{
 uint8_t p = -1;
 lcd.clear();
 lcd.print("Please wait");
 p = finger.deleteModel(id);
 if (p == FINGERPRINT_OK)
 {
  Serial.println("Deleted!");
  lcd.clear();
  lcd.print("Figer Deleted");
  lcd.setCursor(0,1);
  lcd.print("Successfully");
  delay(1000);
 }
 else
 {
  Serial.print("Something Wrong");
  lcd.clear();
  lcd.print("Something Wrong");
  lcd.setCursor(0,1);
```

```
  lcd.print("Try Again Later");
  delay(2000);
  return p;
 }
}
void download(int eepIndex)
{


      if(EEPROM.read(eepIndex)!= 0xff)
    {
     Serial.print("T->");
     if(EEPROM.read(eepIndex)<10)
     Serial.print('0');
     Serial.print(EEPROM.read(eepIndex++));
     Serial.print(':');
     if(EEPROM.read(eepIndex)<10)
     Serial.print('0');
     Serial.print(EEPROM.read(eepIndex++));
     Serial.print(':');
     if(EEPROM.read(eepIndex)<10)
     Serial.print('0');
     Serial.print(EEPROM.read(eepIndex++));
     Serial.print("  D->");
     if(EEPROM.read(eepIndex)<10)
     Serial.print('0');
     Serial.print(EEPROM.read(eepIndex++));
     Serial.print('/');
     if(EEPROM.read(eepIndex)<10)
     Serial.print('0');
     Serial.print(EEPROM.read(eepIndex++));
```

```
    Serial.print('/');
        Serial.print(EEPROM.read(eepIndex++)<<8 |
EEPROM.read(eepIndex++));
    }
    else
    {
     Serial.print("---------------------------");
    }
    Serial.print("   ");
}
```

2. ARDUINO BASED 3-WAY TRAFFIC LIGHT CONTROLLER

We as a whole think about Arduino. It is one of the most famous open source smaller scale controller board which is profoundly helpful for doing DIY ventures. This is a basic Arduino DIY venture which is helpful to comprehend the working of traffic lights we see around us. We have secured an increasingly more straightforward rendition of traffic lights in this rush hour gridlock light circuit. Here have shown it for 3 sides or ways. Presently how about we get into the task...

Components Required:

- 3*Red LED Lights

- 3*Green LED Lights

- Arduino Uno With Ide Cable

- 3*Yellow LED Lights

- Breadboard

- 3*220ohm Resistors

- Male To Male Connectors

Circuit Explanation:

The circuit Diagram for Arduino Traffic Light Controller venture is given beneath:

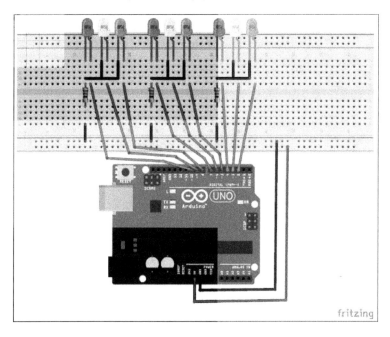

fritzing

It's entirely straightforward and can be effectively based on bread board as clarified in underneath steps:

- Interface the LEDs in the request as Red, Green, and Yellow in the breadboard.

- Spot the negative terminal of the LEDs in like manner and interface the 220ohm resistor in arrangement.

- Interface the connector wires in like manner.

- Interface the opposite finish of the wire to the Arduino Uno in the successive pins(2,3,4... 10)

- Catalyst the breadboard utilizing the Arduino 5v and GND stick.

Program and Working Explanation:

The code for this Arduino Traffic Light Controller Project is basic and can be effectively comprehended. Here we have shown Traffic lights for the 3 different ways street and the code gleams LED's on all the three sides in a specific grouping, where the real Traffic Lights works. Like, at once, there will be two Red flag on any of the different sides and one Green light on the staying side. Furthermore, yellow light will likewise gleam, for 1 second each time, in the middle of change from Red to Green, implies first red light shines for 5 second at that point yellow light sparkles for 1 second and afterward at long last green light will be turned on.

In the program, first we have proclaimed pins (2,3... 10) as yield in void arrangement() for 9 LEDs (three on each side for example forward, both ways side).

```
void setup() {

// configure the output pins

pinMode(2,OUTPUT);
```

```
  pinMode(3,OUTPUT);

  pinMode(4,OUTPUT);

  pinMode(5,OUTPUT);

  pinMode(6,OUTPUT);

  pinMode(7,OUTPUT);

  pinMode(8,OUTPUT);

  pinMode(9,OUTPUT);

  pinMode(10,OUTPUT);

}
```

At that point in void circle() work we have composed the code for traffic lights to be turned on and off in arrangement as referenced previously.

```
void loop()

{

 digitalWrite(2,1); //enables the 1st set of signals

 digitalWrite(7,1);
```

```
digitalWrite(10,1);

digitalWrite(4,0);

digitalWrite(3,0);

digitalWrite(6,0);

digitalWrite(8,0);

digitalWrite(9,0);

digitalWrite(5,0);

delay(5000);

..... ....

..... ....
```

First the upside/forward side is opened (green), while the other different sides (for example left side and right side) stays shut with Red sign, with a deferral of 5 seconds. At that point the yellow light gets turned on at the correct side for 1sec pursued by the Green light, leaving other different sides (for example upside and left side is red) shut with Red Light and 5 seconds deferral. At that point yellow on the left side sparkles for 1sec pursued by green one, leaving upside and right side Red with 5sec postponement. This procedure is circled in void circle() work for ceaseless procedure. Here we can alter delays for which the Red, yellow and Green light stay on and off.

The total Arduino code for this Project is given beneath.

Code

```
void setup() {
// configure the output pins
pinMode(2,OUTPUT);
pinMode(3,OUTPUT);
pinMode(4,OUTPUT);
pinMode(5,OUTPUT);
pinMode(6,OUTPUT);
pinMode(7,OUTPUT);
pinMode(8,OUTPUT);
pinMode(9,OUTPUT);
pinMode(10,OUTPUT);
}
void loop()
{
digitalWrite(2,1); //enables the 1st set of signals
digitalWrite(7,1);
digitalWrite(10,1);
digitalWrite(4,0);
digitalWrite(3,0);
digitalWrite(6,0);
digitalWrite(8,0);
digitalWrite(9,0);
```

```
digitalWrite(5,0);
delay(5000);
digitalWrite(3,1); //enables the yellow lights
digitalWrite(6,1);
digitalWrite(2,0);
digitalWrite(7,0);
delay(1000);
digitalWrite(4,1); //enables the 2nd set of signals
digitalWrite(5,1);
digitalWrite(10,1);
digitalWrite(2,0);
digitalWrite(3,0);
digitalWrite(6,0);
digitalWrite(8,0);
digitalWrite(9,0);
digitalWrite(7,0);
delay(5000);
digitalWrite(9,1); //enables the yellow lights
digitalWrite(6,1);
digitalWrite(10,0);
digitalWrite(5,0);
digitalWrite(4,0);
delay(1000);
digitalWrite(8,1); //enables the 3rd set of signals
digitalWrite(4,1);
digitalWrite(7,1);
digitalWrite(2,0);
digitalWrite(3,0);
digitalWrite(5,0);
digitalWrite(6,0);
digitalWrite(9,0);
```

```
digitalWrite(10,0);
delay(5000);
digitalWrite(9,1); //enables the yellow lights
digitalWrite(3,1);
digitalWrite(7,0);
digitalWrite(8,0);
digitalWrite(4,0);
delay(1000);
}
```

3. ARDUINO BASED ANGRY BIRD GAME CONTROLLER UTILIZING FLEX SENSOR AS WELL AS POTENTIOMETER

It's everything began with a little game from the dim ages called "Mario", directly from the hour of being a minor little person bouncing on ducks to spare my princess till being a manly attractive Prince wandering in Persia (Prince of Persia) battling against dimness to spare my reality behind I have been an extraordinary enthusiast of playing computer games and I grew up playing them. Be that as it may, they do get exhausted up some of the time and I feel less required into it. Today, the propelled gaming consoles empowers virtual gaming and causes us to feel the game significantly more superior to anything a console or a mouse can do.

Being an Arduino Enthusiast I tired playing the renowned game called "Irate Birds" utilizing console and mouse and chose to construct my very own Game Controller utilizing a Flex Sensor as well as a Potentiometer. At the point when the flex sensor is pulled the feathered creature on the sling will likewise be pulled and you can utilize the potentiometer to set the heading wherein it ought to be propelled. At that point when you discharge the flex sensor the flying creature will be propelled. I practically appreciated doing it, so on the off chance that you are up to structure something fundamentally the same as, at that point this instructional exercise will be a useful. This instructional exercise will likewise be useful in Controlling Mouse Cursor utilizing Potentiometer.

Software and Hardware Requirements:

Programming:
- Handling IDE

- Arduino IDE

- Furious Birds Game on Computer

Equipment:

- Flex Sensor

- Arduino (Any Version)

- Potentiometer

- Interfacing Wires

- 47K ohm Resistor

- Breadboard

Flex Sensor

Concept Behind:

The Arduino Board peruses the qualities from the Potentiometer and Flex Senor and Transmits them to the Laptop/PC through USB COM port by means of ordinary Serial.write() work. We at that point read this data utilizing Processing and control the mouse cursor utilizing the Robot class in Java which is upheld by handling IDE. We have modified the handling IDE so that when the Flex sensor is pulled a mouse snap will be made and dependent on the amount it is pulled the mouse pointer will move in X heading. At that point dependent on the incentive from potentiometer we will move the mouse cursor in Y heading, thusly we can set the course wherein feathered creature ought to be propelled.

Circuit Diagram:

The circuit for playing the Angry Bird utilizing Flex Sensor as well as Potentiometer is simple.

We have basic associated a potentiometer and a flex sensor to the Analog information sources (A0,A1) of the Arduino. The yield of the Flex sensor is likewise pulled down utilizing a 47K draw down resistor.

You can legitimately associate it on breadboard or weld them to a Perf board and collect it on a gloves or something to make it increasingly inventive. I have essentially utilized a breadboard to do my associations as demonstrated as follows:

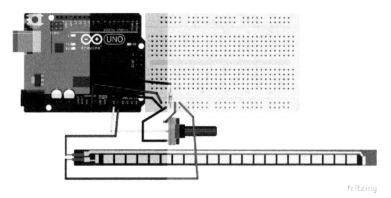

Arduino Program:

The total Arduino code is given toward the finish of the instructional exercise. Barely any significant lines are clarified beneath.

We instate the program to work with 9600 baud rate and start perusing the qualities from Flex sensor and Potentiometer. As we probably am aware serial. write() capacity can send just a single byte of information at once. Since One byte is 8 bits and $2^8 = 256$. We will have the option to send esteems from 0 to 256. So we need to pack the estimations of Flex sensor yield and Potentiometer Output into 0 to 256.

To do that we utilize the guide() work in Arduino. Every one of the qualities from the flex sensor are changed over from 5 to 100, so when we twist the sensor it will increase from 5 and when discharged it will return to 5. To make reference to the mouse taps the worth 1 and 0 is utilized. At the point when 1 is sent the mouse is squeezed and when 0 is sent the mouse is discharged.

```
if (FlexValue>=65 && FlexValue<=120) //my flex
sensor varies from 65 to 120, your might be differ-
ent

 {

 FlexValue = map (FlexValue,120,65,0,100);   //
based on bending convert to 0 to 100

 if(FlexValue>=5) // 1 and 0 is used for mouse click
so start from 5

 {

 Mclick=true;

 Serial.write(1);  //1 is sent to make mouse left
click

 Serial.write(FlexValue); //Flex value is the dis-
tance to move mouse in X direction

 }

 else
```

```
{

Mclick=false;

Serial.write(0);}

}
```

So also the qualities structure the potentiometer is changed over from 101 to 200 sing the guide() work and is send to the Laptops COM port suing the Serial. write() work as demonstrated as follows.

```
if(potValue<=200)

{

  potValue  =  map(potValue,0,200,101,201);  // Based in turn convert to 101 to 201

  Serial.write(potValue); //Pot value is the distance to move mouse in Y direction

}
```

Preparing Code:

Preparing is an Open-Source advancement application and can be effectively downloaded and put to use for creating intriguing activities utilizing Arduino or different Microcontrollers. We have just completed couple of activities utilizing Processing and you can look at them by tapping on the connections underneath.

- DIY FM Radio Using Processing

- Computer generated Reality/Gesture control utilizing Arduino

- Private Chat room utilizing Arduino.

- Arduino Radar System utilizing Processing APP as well as Ultrasonic Sensor

- Constant Face Detection as well as Tracking utilizing Arduino

- DIY Speedometer utilizing Arduino and Processing

- Ping Pong Game utilizing Arduino Accelerometer

- Biped Robot Using Arduino

- DIY Arduino Thermal Imaging Camera

In this venture we have utilized the handling IDE to peruse the COM port qualities and control the mouse pointer dependent on the qualities got by means of the COM port. The total Processing Code for this Angry Bird Game Controller can be downloaded from the beneath connect:

- Handling Code for this Angry Bird Game Controller (right Click and 'Spare connection as')

Arduino Program can be found toward the finish of this instructional exercise. The Processing code was altered to fit for our motivation from the code given by yoggy on his GitHub page.

The information originating from the COM port ought to be perused in a similar baud rate in which it was sent from Arduino. Likewise check which COM port your Arduino is associated by utilizing the gadget chief. My Arduino was associated with COM3 and it was the 0th Port in my PC and the baud rate in Arduino was 9600 so the code is as per the following

```
port = new Serial(this,Serial.list()[0],9600);
```

When we start perusing the qualities we recognize it by remembering it dependent on its incentive on how we sent from Arduino. The qualities are again mapped from 0 to 100 with the goal that we will have the option to control the mouse situated in that worth.

```
if(port.available()>0)

 {

  data=port.read();

   println(data); //Read the data from COM port and
save it in data

 }

 if(data>=101 && data<=201) //If the value if from
101 to 201 then it must be from Potentiometer

 {

   Turn = int (map (data,101,201,0,100)); //Use
that value to turn the catapullt

 }

 if(data>=5 && data <=100) //If the value if from 5
to 100 then it must be from Flex Sensor

 { Pull = int (map(data,5,100,0,100));} //Use that
value to pull the catapult

 if(data == 1)
```

```
click = true; //Use that value to press the mouse
button

if (data == 0)

click = false; //Use that value to release the mouse
button
```

When we classify the information we would then be able to control the mouse utilizing the Robot Java Class in Processing. The direction robot. mouseMove(crntX-Pull, crntY+Turn); can be utilized to move the mouse to any ideal position and the lines robot.mousePress(InputEvent.BUTTON1_DOWN_MASK); and robot.mouseRelease(InputEvent.BUTTON1_DOWN_MASK); can be utilized to press or discharge the mouse button individually.

```
if (click == false) //when Flex Sesnor is not pulled

{

crntX = (int)p.getX(); crntY = (int)p.getY();

if (Pull > 50)

robot.mouseRelease(InputEvent.BUTTON1_
DOWN_MASK); //Release the mouse button
```

```
    }

    if(click == true) //when Flex Sesnor is pulled

    {

      robot.mousePress(InputEvent.BUTTON1_
    DOWN_MASK); //Press the mouse Button

      robot.mouseMove(crntX-Pull,  crntY+Turn); //
    Move the mouse based on the Flex and POT value

    }

}
```

The handling IDE when propelled will likewise show a little exchange Box on which you can discover the estimations of Pull, Turn and status of Mouse Click as demonstrated as follows

This detail can be utilized to troubleshoot the Program or right any information required.

Working:

To irritate Bird Project work utilizing the code gave, amass your equipment as indicated by the circuit chart and transfer the given Arduino Code. At that point Note which COM port your Arduino is associated with and make the vital changes in the Processing code and dispatch the preparing sketch.

Presently, just dispatch the irate winged creature game and spot you cursor close to the launch and destroy the flex sensor to pull the fowl and set the heading utilizing the potentiometer. When the course is set discharge the Flex sensor

EEEEWWWWWEEEEEEEEEE!!!!!!!!!!...............

You fledgling will be hurled directly into the air and BOOMM!! On the piggies.

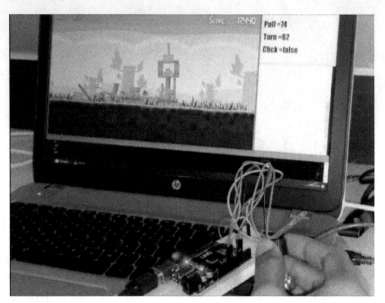

Expectation you appreciated the task and had the option to assemble something comparable.

Presently, time to collide with those piggy boxes and get back our fowls eggs!!!!

Code

```
/*
* Angry Bird Game Controller Program
*/
void setup() {
 Serial.begin(9600); //Transmit at 9600 Baud Rate
}
boolean Mclick = false;
```

```
void loop() {
  int potValue = analogRead(A0); //variable to store
potValue
  int FlexValue = analogRead(A1); //variable to store
Flex Value
// Serial.println(FlexValue);
// Serial.print("POT: ");
// Serial.println(potValue);
// Serial.print("Flex: ");
   if (FlexValue>=65 && FlexValue<=115) //my flex
sensor varies from 65 to 120, your might be different
 {
  FlexValue = map (FlexValue,120,65,0,100); //based
on bending convert to 0 to 100


  if (FlexValue>=5) // 1 and 0 is used for mouse click
so start from 5
 {
 Mclick=true;
 Serial.write(1); //1 is sent to make mouse left click
  Serial.write(FlexValue); //Flex value is the distance
to move mouse in X direction
 }
 else
 {
 Mclick=false;
 Serial.write(0);}
 }
 else
 {
```

```
Mclick=false;
Serial.write(0);}


if(potValue<=200)
{
  potValue = map(potValue,0,200,101,201); //Based
in turn convert to 101 to 201
  Serial.write(potValue); //Pot value is the distance to
move mouse in Y direction
}
  delay(500);   //stability delay
}
```

4. UNIQUE MARK BASED BIOMETRIC VOTING MACHINE UTILIZING ARDUINO

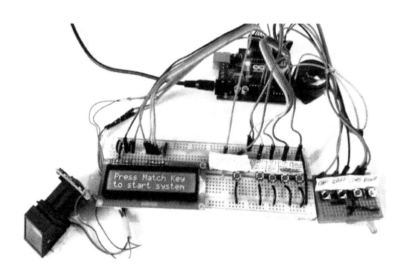

We as a whole are very acquainted with Electronic Voting Machines, where your vote gets enrolled electronically and you don't have to utilize voting form paper to cast a ballot in political race. Today security is a significant concern and it likewise should be guaranteed that somebody can't cast a ballot twice, so this issue can be illuminated by presenting Finger

Print Based Voting, where an individual can be approved dependent on his unique finger impression. This will likewise stops phony democratic.

Likewise check our past Electronic Voting Machine Projects utilizing distinctive Microcontrollers:

- Electronic Voting Machine utilizing Raspberry Pi

- RFID Based Voting Machine

- AVR Microcontroller Based Electronic Voting Machine Project

- Electronic Voting Machine utilizing Arduino

Required Components:

- Arduino Uno
- Finger Print Sensor Module
- Push Buttons
- LEDs -2
- 1K Resistor -3
- 2.2K resistor
- Connecting wires
- Bread Board
- Power
- 16x2 LCD
- Buzzer

Finger Print Sensor Module in Voting Machine:

Unique finger impression Sensor Module or Finger Print Scanner is a module which catches finger impression picture and afterward changes over it into the proportional format and spares them into its memory on chose ID (area) by Arduino. Here all the procedure is instructed by Arduino like taking a picture of unique finger impression, convert it into formats and putting away area and so forth.

In this FingerPrint Voting Machine Circuit, we have utilized Finger Print Sensor Module to validate genuine voter by taking their finger contribution to the framework. Here we are using 5 push catches to Match, Enroll/back, Delete/OK, UP and Down. Enlist and Del key have twofold highlights here. Enlist key is utilized for selecting new finger impression into the framework and back capacity too. Means when the client requires to select new finger then he/she needs to press enlist key then LCD requests the ID or Location where client have to store the rare finger impression yield. Presently in case as of now client would prefer not to continue further, at that point he/she can press enlist key again to return (this time select key carry on as Back key). Means select key has both enlistment and back capacity. DEL/OK key likewise has same twofold capacity like when client enlists new finger then he/she have to choose finger ID or Location by utilizing another two key in particular UP AND DOWN now client needs to press DEL/OK key (this time this key carries on like OK) to continue with chosen ID or Location. Match key is utilized for at whatever point voter needs to cast a ballot then he/she needs to confirm first for genuine voter by keeping finger on Finger Print Sensor, on the off chance that he/she went in this validation then he/she can cast a ballot.

To get familiar with selecting fingerprints and different things, Check our past instructional exercise on interfacing Finger Print Sensor with Arduino.

Working Explanation:

Working of this Biometric Voting System for Election is somewhat perplexing for learners. Above all else, client needs to enlist finger or voters (in this code max point of confinement of the voter is 25) with the assistance of push catches/keys. To do this client need to press ENROLL key and afterward LCD requests entering area/ID where finger will be a store. So now client needs to enter ID (Location) by spending/DOWN keys. Subsequent to choosing Location/ID client needs to press an OK key (DEL key). Presently LCD will request putting finger over the unique mark module. Presently client have to put his finger over unique mark module. At that point LCD will request to expel the finger from unique mark module as well as again request putting the finger. Presently client needs to put his finger again over unique finger impression module. Presently unique finger impression module takes a picture and changes over it into formats and stores it by chose ID in to the finger impression module's memory. Presently voter will be enrolled and he/she can cast a ballot. By same technique all the voter can be enlisted into the framework.

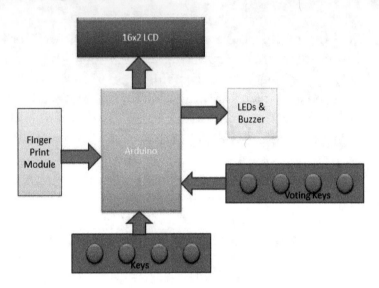

Presently in case the client needs to expel or erase any of put away ID, at that point he/she have to press DEL key, subsequent to squeezing DEL key, LCD will request select area means select ID that to be erased. Presently client needs to choose ID and press OK key (same DEL key). Presently LCD will tell you that finger has erased effectively.

Voting Process:

Presently when client needs to cast a ballot then he/she needs to press match key and after that ringer will signal and LED will likewise shine and LCD will request spot finger over unique mark module. Presently Arduino will give you three endeavors to put your finger. Subsequent to setting a finger over unique finger impression module unique mark module catches finger picture discover its IDs is available in the framework. On the off chance that finger ID distinguished, at that point LCD will show approved Voter. It implies the client is approved to cast a ballot. And after that the framework moves to next stage for casting a ballot. Presently Green LED will shine it implies now voter can decide in favor of their applicants by squeezing a relected key (from RED bread board in this show). Presently in case a similar voter needs to cast a ballot once more, at that point the framework will show it 'As of now Voted'. Means same voter can't cast a ballot again and signal will blare for 5 seconds. On the off chance that any Non-enrolled client needs to cast a ballot, at that point unique mark module won't identify its ID into the framework and LCD will show 'No Fingerprint Found'.

CAN1, CAN2, CAN3 here speaks to the Candidate 1, Candidate 2 and Candidate 3, who have represented political decision.

Circuit Explanation:

The circuit of this FingerPrint Based Voting Machine Project is basic which contains Arduino for controlling entire the procedure of the venture, push button for enlisting, erasing, choosing IDs and casting a ballot reason, a signal for alert, LEDs for sign and 16x2 LCD for train Voter and demonstrating the outcome too. Yellow LED demonstrates that unique finger impression module is prepared to take a picture of the finger and Green LED shows that framework is prepared to take a vote or get results.

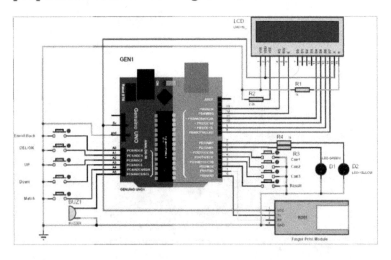

The push catch is straightforwardly associated with stick A0(ENROL), A1(DEL), A2(UP), A3(DOWN) and A4(Match), D5(Can1), D4(Can2), D3(Can3), D2(Result) of Arduino concerning ground. Yellow LED is associated at Digital stick D7 of Arduino concerning ground through a 1k resistor and Green LED is associated with D6 of Arduino with a similar strategy. Unique mark module's Rx and Tx straightforwardly associated at Serial stick Tx and Rx of Arduino. 5v supply is utilized for driving unique mark module taken from Arduino board. A signal is additionally associated at A5. A 16x2 LCD is arranged in 4-piece mode and its RS, EN, D4, D5, D6, and D7 are straightforwardly associated at Digital stick D13, D12, D11, D10, D9, and D8 of Arduino.

Program Explanation:

In a program, we have utilized Adafruit Fingerprint Sensor Library for interfacing unique mark module with Arduino board. You can check the total Code underneath. Here we are clarifying fundamental elements of the Arduino Program.

In arrangement work, we have offered headings to characterized sticks and have started the LCD and Fingerprint module.

After it, in void circle() work, we have sat tight for check key and press Match key to begin the unique finger impression to take information and contrast caught picture id and put away IDs. On the off chance that a match happens, at that point continue with following stage.

```
void loop()

{

lcd.setCursor(0,0);

lcd.print("Press Match Key ");

lcd.setCursor(0,1);

lcd.print("to start system");

digitalWrite(indVote, LOW);

digitalWrite(indFinger, LOW);

if(digitalRead(match)==0)

{

  digitalWrite(buzzer, HIGH);

  delay(200);

  digitalWrite(buzzer, LOW);

  digitalWrite(indFinger, HIGH);
```

```
for(int i=0;i<3;i++)

..... .....

....... ....
```

Given void checkKeys() work is utilized for checking Enroll or DEL key is squeezed or not and what to do whenever squeezed. In the event that the Enroll key squeezed the Enroll() work is called and DEL key press at that point erase() work is called.

```
void checkKeys()

{

  if(digitalRead(enroll) == 0)

  {

  lcd.clear();

  lcd.print("Please Wait");

  delay(1000);

  while(digitalRead(enroll) == 0);

  Enroll();
```

```
}

else if(digitalRead(del) == 0)

{

lcd.clear();

lcd.print("Please Wait");

delay(1000);

delet();

 }

}
```

Given capacity is utilized for entering ID to be erased and calling uint8_t deleteFingerprint(uint8_t id) work that will erase finger from records.

```
void delet()

{

  int count=0;

  lcd.clear();
```

```
lcd.print("Delete Finger  ");

lcd.setCursor(0,1);

lcd.print("Location:");

while(1)

{

  lcd.setCursor(9,1);

  lcd.print(count);

  if(digitalRead(up) == 0)

  {

    count++;

    if(count>25)

    count=0;

    delay(500);

  }
.... .....
```

....

Given capacity is utilized for erase unique mark from the record of chosen ID.

```
uint8_t deleteFingerprint(uint8_t id)

{

  uint8_t p = -1;

  lcd.clear();

  lcd.print("Please wait");

  p = finger.deleteModel(id);

  if(p == FINGERPRINT_OK)

  {

    Serial.println("Deleted!");

    lcd.clear();

    lcd.print("Figer Deleted");

    lcd.setCursor(0,1);
```

```
    lcd.print("Successfully");

    delay(1000);

  }

  else

  {

    Serial.print("Something Wrong");

    lcd.clear();

    lcd.print("Something Wrong");

    lcd.setCursor(0,1);

    lcd.print("Try Again Later");

    delay(2000);

    return p;

  }

}
```

Given Function is used to taking finger print image

and convert them into the template and save it by selected ID into the finger print module memory.

```
uint8_t getFingerprintEnroll()

{

  int p = -1;

  lcd.clear();

  lcd.print("finger ID:");

  lcd.print(id);

  lcd.setCursor(0,1);

  lcd.print("Place Finger");

  delay(2000);

  while (p != FINGERPRINT_OK)

  {

    p = finger.getImage();

..... .....

........ ....
```

Given capacity is utilized for Voting and show results:

```
void Vote()

{

  lcd.clear();

  lcd.print("Please Place");

  lcd.setCursor(0,1);

  lcd.print("Your Vote");

  digitalWrite(indVote, HIGH);

  digitalWrite(indFinger, LOW);

  digitalWrite(buzzer, HIGH);

  delay(500);

  digitalWrite(buzzer, LOW);

  delay(1000);

  while(1)

  {
```

```
    if(digitalRead(sw1)==0)

..... .....

........ ....
```

Check the Full Code Below.

Code

```
#include<EEPROM.h>
#include<LiquidCrystal.h>
LiquidCrystal lcd(13,12,11,10,9,8);
#include <Adafruit_Fingerprint.h>
uint8_t id;
Adafruit_Fingerprint finger = Adafruit_Fingerprint(&Serial);
#define enroll 14
#define del 15
#define up 16
#define down 17
#define match 18
#define indVote 6
#define sw1 5
#define sw2 4
#define sw3 3
#define resultsw 2
#define indFinger 7
#define buzzer 19
#define records 25
int vote1,vote2,vote3;
```

```
int flag;
void setup()
{
  delay(1000);
  pinMode(enroll, INPUT_PULLUP);
  pinMode(up, INPUT_PULLUP);
  pinMode(down, INPUT_PULLUP);
  pinMode(del, INPUT_PULLUP);
  pinMode(match, INPUT_PULLUP);
  pinMode(sw1, INPUT_PULLUP);
  pinMode(sw2, INPUT_PULLUP);
  pinMode(sw3, INPUT_PULLUP);
  pinMode(resultsw, INPUT_PULLUP);
  pinMode(buzzer, OUTPUT);
  pinMode(indVote, OUTPUT);
  pinMode(indFinger, OUTPUT);
lcd.begin(16,2);
 if(digitalRead(resultsw) ==0)
 {
   for(int i=0;i<records;i++)
    EEPROM.write(i+10,0xff);
   EEPROM.write(0,0);
   EEPROM.write(1,0);
   EEPROM.write(2,0);
   lcd.clear();
   lcd.print("System Reset");
   delay(1000);
 }
  lcd.clear();
  lcd.print("Voting Machine");
  lcd.setCursor(0,1);
```

```
lcd.print("by Finger Print");
delay(2000);
lcd.clear();
lcd.print("Hello World");
lcd.setCursor(0,1);
lcd.print("Saddam Khan");
delay(2000);
if(EEPROM.read(0) == 0xff)
EEPROM.write(0,0);
if(EEPROM.read(1) == 0xff)
EEPROM.write(1,0);
if(EEPROM.read(1) == 0xff)
EEPROM.write(1,0);
//finger.begin(57600);
Serial.begin(57600);
lcd.clear();
lcd.print("Finding Module");
lcd.setCursor(0,1);
delay(1000);
if(finger.verifyPassword())
{
  //Serial.println("Found fingerprint sensor!");
  lcd.clear();
  lcd.print("Found Module ");
  delay(1000);
}
else
{
//Serial.println("Did not find fingerprint sensor :(");
lcd.clear();
lcd.print("module not Found");
```

```
 lcd.setCursor(0,1);
 lcd.print("Check Connections");
 while (1);
 }
lcd.clear();
lcd.setCursor(0,0);
lcd.print("Cn1");
lcd.setCursor(4,0);
lcd.print("Cn2");
lcd.setCursor(8,0);
lcd.print("Cn3");
lcd.setCursor(12,0);
lcd.print("Cn4");
lcd.setCursor(0,1);
vote1=EEPROM.read(0);
lcd.print(vote1);
 lcd.setCursor(6,1);
vote2=EEPROM.read(1);
lcd.print(vote2);
lcd.setCursor(12,1);
vote3=EEPROM.read(2);
lcd.print(vote3);
delay(2000);
}
void loop()
{
lcd.setCursor(0,0);
lcd.print("Press Match Key ");
lcd.setCursor(0,1);
lcd.print("to start system");
digitalWrite(indVote, LOW);
```

```
digitalWrite(indFinger, LOW);
if(digitalRead(match)==0)
{
digitalWrite(buzzer, HIGH);
delay(200);
digitalWrite(buzzer, LOW);
digitalWrite(indFinger, HIGH);
for(int i=0;i<3;i++)
{
 lcd.clear();
 lcd.print("Place Finger");
 delay(2000);
 int result=getFingerprintIDez();
 if(result>=0)
 {
  flag=0;
   for(int i=0;i<records;i++)
   {
    if(result == EEPROM.read(i+10))
    {
     lcd.clear();
     lcd.print("Authorised Voter");
     lcd.setCursor(0,1);
     lcd.print("Please Wait....");
     delay(1000);
     Vote();
     EEPROM.write(i+10, 0xff);
     flag=1;
     return;
    }
   }
```

```
if(flag == 0)
{
lcd.clear();
lcd.print("Already Voted");
//lcd.setCursor(0,1);
//lcd.print("")
digitalWrite(buzzer, HIGH);
delay(5000);
digitalWrite(buzzer, LOW);
return;
}
}
}
lcd.clear();
}
checkKeys();
delay(1000);
}
void checkKeys()
{
if(digitalRead(enroll) == 0)
{
lcd.clear();
lcd.print("Please Wait");
delay(1000);
while(digitalRead(enroll) == 0);
Enroll();
}
else if(digitalRead(del) == 0)
{
lcd.clear();
```

```
  lcd.print("Please Wait");
  delay(1000);
  delet();
  }
}
void Enroll()
{
 int count=0;
 lcd.clear();
 lcd.print("Enter Finger ID:");
 while(1)
 {
 lcd.setCursor(0,1);
  lcd.print(count);
  if(digitalRead(up) == 0)
  {
   count++;
   if(count>25)
   count=0;
   delay(500);
  }
  else if(digitalRead(down) == 0)
  {
   count--;
   if(count<0)
   count=25;
   delay(500);
  }
  else if(digitalRead(del) == 0)
  {
    id=count;
```

```
    getFingerprintEnroll();
    for(int i=0;i<records;i++)
    {
     if(EEPROM.read(i+10) == 0xff)
     {
      EEPROM.write(i+10, id);
      break;
     }
    }
    return;
   }
    else if(digitalRead(enroll) == 0)
   {
     return;
   }
 }
}
void delet()
{
 int count=0;
 lcd.clear();
 lcd.print("Enter Finger ID");
 while(1)
 {
 lcd.setCursor(0,1);
  lcd.print(count);
  if(digitalRead(up) == 0)
  {
   count++;
   if(count>25)
   count=0;
```

```
  delay(500);
 }
 else if(digitalRead(down) == 0)
 {
  count--;
  if(count<0)
  count=25;
  delay(500);
 }
 else if(digitalRead(del) == 0)
 {
   id=count;
   deleteFingerprint(id);
   for(int i=0;i<records;i++)
   {
    if(EEPROM.read(i+10) == id)
    {
     EEPROM.write(i+10,0xff);
     break;
    }
   }
   return;
 }
  else if(digitalRead(enroll) == 0)
  {
    return;
  }
}
}
uint8_t getFingerprintEnroll()
{
```

```
int p = -1;
lcd.clear();
lcd.print("finger ID:");
lcd.print(id);
lcd.setCursor(0,1);
lcd.print("Place Finger");
delay(2000);
while (p != FINGERPRINT_OK)
{
 p = finger.getImage();
 switch (p)
 {
 case FINGERPRINT_OK:
  //Serial.println("Image taken");
  lcd.clear();
  lcd.print("Image taken");
  break;
 case FINGERPRINT_NOFINGER:
  //Serial.println("No Finger");
  lcd.clear();
  lcd.print("No Finger");
  break;
 case FINGERPRINT_PACKETRECIEVEERR:
  //Serial.println("Communication error");
  lcd.clear();
  lcd.print("Comm Error");
  break;
 case FINGERPRINT_IMAGEFAIL:
  //Serial.println("Imaging error");
  lcd.clear();
  lcd.print("Imaging Error");
```

```
  break;
 default:
  //Serial.println("Unknown error");
  lcd.clear();
  lcd.print("Unknown Error");
  break;
 }
}
// OK success!
p = finger.image2Tz(1);
switch (p) {
 case FINGERPRINT_OK:
  //Serial.println("Image converted");
  lcd.clear();
  lcd.print("Image converted");
  break;
 case FINGERPRINT_IMAGEMESS:
  //Serial.println("Image too messy");
  lcd.clear();
  lcd.print("Image too messy");
  return p;
 case FINGERPRINT_PACKETRECIEVEERR:
  //Serial.println("Communication error");
    lcd.clear();
  lcd.print("Comm Error");
  return p;
 case FINGERPRINT_FEATUREFAIL:
    //Serial.println("Could not find fingerprint features");
    lcd.clear();
  lcd.print("Feature Not Found");
```

```
   return p;
 case FINGERPRINT_INVALIDIMAGE:
     //Serial.println("Could not find fingerprint fea-
tures");
       lcd.clear();
  lcd.print("Feature Not Found");
  return p;
 default:
  //Serial.println("Unknown error");
      lcd.clear();
  lcd.print("Unknown Error");
  return p;
}
//Serial.println("Remove finger");
lcd.clear();
lcd.print("Remove Finger");
delay(2000);
p = 0;
while (p != FINGERPRINT_NOFINGER) {
 p = finger.getImage();
}
//Serial.print("ID "); //Serial.println(id);
p = -1;
//Serial.println("Place same finger again");
lcd.clear();
  lcd.print("Place Finger");
  lcd.setCursor(0,1);
  lcd.print("  Again");
while (p != FINGERPRINT_OK) {
 p = finger.getImage();
 switch (p) {
```

```
 case FINGERPRINT_OK:
  //Serial.println("Image taken");
  break;
 case FINGERPRINT_NOFINGER:
  //Serial.print(".");
  break;
 case FINGERPRINT_PACKETRECIEVEERR:
  //Serial.println("Communication error");
  break;
 case FINGERPRINT_IMAGEFAIL:
  //Serial.println("Imaging error");
  break;
 default:
  //Serial.println("Unknown error");
  return;
 }
}
// OK success!
p = finger.image2Tz(2);
switch (p) {
 case FINGERPRINT_OK:
  //Serial.println("Image converted");
  break;
 case FINGERPRINT_IMAGEMESS:
  //Serial.println("Image too messy");
  return p;
 case FINGERPRINT_PACKETRECIEVEERR:
  //Serial.println("Communication error");
  return p;
 case FINGERPRINT_FEATUREFAIL:
     //Serial.println("Could not find fingerprint fea-
```

```
tures");
  return p;
 case FINGERPRINT_INVALIDIMAGE:
     //Serial.println("Could not find fingerprint fea-
tures");
  return p;
 default:
  //Serial.println("Unknown error");
  return p;
}
// OK converted!
  //Serial.print("Creating model for #");  //Serial.
println(id);
 p = finger.createModel();
 if (p == FINGERPRINT_OK) {
  //Serial.println("Prints matched!");
 } else if (p == FINGERPRINT_PACKETRECIEVEERR) {
  //Serial.println("Communication error");
  return p;
 } else if (p == FINGERPRINT_ENROLLMISMATCH) {
  //Serial.println("Fingerprints did not match");
  return p;
 } else {
  //Serial.println("Unknown error");
  return p;
 }
//Serial.print("ID "); //Serial.println(id);
 p = finger.storeModel(id);
 if (p == FINGERPRINT_OK) {
  //Serial.println("Stored!");
```

```
 lcd.clear();
 lcd.print("Stored!");
 delay(2000);
} else if (p == FINGERPRINT_PACKETRECIEVEERR) {
 //Serial.println("Communication error");
 return p;
} else if (p == FINGERPRINT_BADLOCATION) {
 //Serial.println("Could not store in that location");
 return p;
} else if (p == FINGERPRINT_FLASHERR) {
 //Serial.println("Error writing to flash");
 return p;
}
else {
 //Serial.println("Unknown error");
 return p;
}
}
int getFingerprintIDez()
{
 uint8_t p = finger.getImage();
 if (p != FINGERPRINT_OK)
 return -1;
 p = finger.image2Tz();
 if (p != FINGERPRINT_OK)
 return -1;
 p = finger.fingerFastSearch();
 if (p != FINGERPRINT_OK)
 {
 lcd.clear();
 lcd.print("Finger Not Found");
```

```
lcd.setCursor(0,1);
lcd.print("Try Later");
delay(2000);
return -1;
}
// found a match!
//Serial.print("Found ID #");
//Serial.print(finger.fingerID);
return finger.fingerID;
}
uint8_t deleteFingerprint(uint8_t id)
{
uint8_t p = -1;
lcd.clear();
lcd.print("Please wait");
p = finger.deleteModel(id);
if (p == FINGERPRINT_OK)
{
//Serial.println("Deleted!");
lcd.clear();
lcd.print("Figer Deleted");
lcd.setCursor(0,1);
lcd.print("Successfully");
delay(1000);
}
else
{
//Serial.print("Something Wrong");
lcd.clear();
lcd.print("Something Wrong");
lcd.setCursor(0,1);
```

```
 lcd.print("Try Again Later");
 delay(2000);
 return p;
}
}
void Vote()
{
 lcd.clear();
 lcd.print("Please Place");
 lcd.setCursor(0,1);
 lcd.print("Your Vote");
 digitalWrite(indVote, HIGH);
 digitalWrite(indFinger, LOW);
 digitalWrite(buzzer, HIGH);
 delay(500);
 digitalWrite(buzzer, LOW);
 delay(1000);
 while(1)
 {
    if(digitalRead(sw1)==0)
    {
     vote1++;
     voteSubmit(1);
     EEPROM.write(0, vote1);
     while(digitalRead(sw1)==0);
     return;
    }
    if(digitalRead(sw2)==0)
    {
     vote2++;
      voteSubmit(2);
```

```
 EEPROM.write(1, vote2);
 while(digitalRead(sw2)==0);
 return;
}
if(digitalRead(sw3)==0)
{
 vote3++;
  voteSubmit(3);
  EEPROM.write(2, vote3);
 while(digitalRead(sw3)==0);
 return;
}
 if(digitalRead(resultsw)==0)
 {
  lcd.clear();
  lcd.setCursor(0,0);
  lcd.print("Can1");
  lcd.setCursor(6,0);
  lcd.print("Can2");
  lcd.setCursor(12,0);
  lcd.print("Can3");
  for(int i=0;i<3;i++)
  {
   lcd.setCursor(i*6,1);
   lcd.print(EEPROM.read(i));
  }
  delay(2000);
 int vote=vote1+vote2+vote3;
 if(vote)
 {
 if((vote1 > vote2 && vote1 > vote3))
```

```
{
lcd.clear();
lcd.print("Can1 Wins");
delay(2000);
lcd.clear();
}
else if(vote2 > vote1 && vote2 > vote3)
{
lcd.clear();
lcd.print("Can2 Wins");
delay(2000);
lcd.clear();
}
else if((vote3 > vote1 && vote3 > vote2))
{
lcd.clear();
lcd.print("Can3 Wins");
delay(2000);
lcd.clear();
}
else
{
lcd.clear();
lcd.print("  Tie Up Or  ");
lcd.setCursor(0,1);
lcd.print("  No Result  ");
delay(1000);
lcd.clear();
}
}
else
```

```
   {
    lcd.clear();
    lcd.print("No Voting....");
    delay(1000);
    lcd.clear();
   }
   vote1=0;vote2=0;vote3=0;vote=0;
   lcd.clear();
   return;
   }
 }
  digitalWrite(indVote, LOW);
}
void voteSubmit(int cn)
{
 lcd.clear();
 if(cn == 1)
   lcd.print("Can1");
 else if(cn == 2)
   lcd.print("Can2");
 else if(cn == 3)
   lcd.print("Can3");
 lcd.setCursor(0,1);
 lcd.print("Vote Submitted");
 digitalWrite(buzzer , HIGH);
 delay(1000);
 digitalWrite(buzzer, LOW);
 digitalWrite(indVote, LOW);
 return;
}
```

5. BIOMETRIC SECURITY SYSTEM UTILIZING ARDUINO AND FINGERPRINT SENSOR

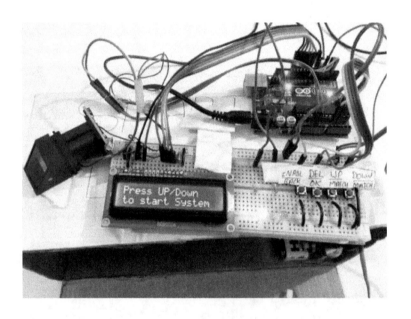

Security is a significant worry in our everyday life, and computerized locks have turned into a important piece of these security frameworks. There are numerous sorts of security frameworks accessible to verify our place. A few models are PIR based Security System, RFID based Security System, Digital Lock System, bio-framework frameworks, Electronics Code lock. Here we will Interface a Fingerprint Sensor Module with Arduino as well as will assemble a Fingerprint based Biometric Security System with entryway locking. Unique mark is viewed as the most secure key to bolt or open any framework as it can perceive any individual particularly and can't be replicated effectively.

Components Required:

- Arduino Uno
- Finger Print Module
- Push Button -4
- LEDs -2
- 1K Resistor -3
- 2.2K resistor -1 `
- Power Supply
- Connecting wires
- Cardboard Box
- Servo Motor -1
- 16x2 LCD -1
- Bread Board -1

Finger Print Sensor Module with Arduino:

Unique finger impression Sensor Module or Finger Print Scanner is a module which catches unique mark picture and afterward changes over it into the proportional layout and spares them into its memory on chose ID (area) by Arduino. Here all the procedure is told by Arduino like taking a picture of unique finger impression, convert it into formats and putting away area and so on.

In this Arduino Fingerprint Sensor Project, we have utilized Fingerprint Sensor Module to take finger or thumb impression as contribution to the framework. Here we are utilizing 4 drive catches to Enroll/back, Delete/OK, UP and Down. Each key has twofold highlights. Enlist key is utilized for selecting new finger impression into the framework and back capacity also. Means when the client have to select new finger then he/she needs to press enlist key then LCD requests the ID or Location where client needs to store the unique finger impression yield. Presently in case as of now client would prefer not to continue further, at that point he/she can press select key again to return (this time enlist key carry on as Back key). Means enlist key has both enlistment and back capacity. DEL/OK key likewise has same twofold capacity like when client enlists new finger then he/she have to choose finger ID or Location by using another two key to be specific UP/MATCH AND DOWN/MATCH (which additionally has twofold capacity) presently client needs to press DEL/OK key (this time this key acts like OK) to continue with chosen ID or Location. UP/DOWN keys additionally bolster Finger print match work.

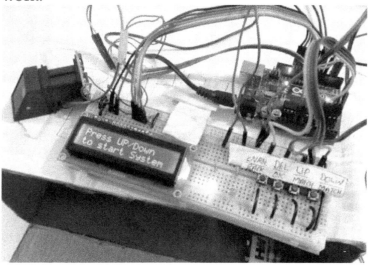

Here we have additionally joined a cardboard box with a Servo Motor to go about as a security entryway, which will possibly open when the framework will peruse right Finger Print. Yellow LED shows door is shut and Green LED demonstrates entryway is opened.

Working Explanation:

Working of this Fingerprint Sensor Door Lock is simple. In this venture, we have utilized an entryway that will be open when we spot put away finger at the unique finger impression module. As a matter of first importance, the client needs to select finger with the assistance of push button/keys. To do this press ENROLL key as well as after that LCD requests entering area/ID where finger will be a store. So now client needs to enter ID (Location) by spending/ DOWN keys. In the wake of choosing Location/ID client needs to press an OK key (DEL key). Presently LCD will request setting finger over the unique mark module. Presently client have to put his finger over unique mark module. At that point LCD will request to expel the finger from unique mark module as well as again request putting the finger. Presently to put finger again over unique mark module. Presently unique mark module takes a picture as well as changes over it into layouts as well as stores it by chose ID in to the finger impression module's memory. Presently client can open the entryway by setting a similar finger that he/she have included or selected into the framework and after that press MATCH key (UP/Down key). By a similar strategy, the client can include more fingers.

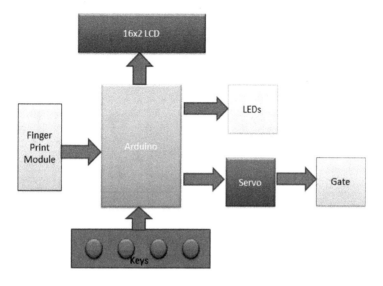

Presently in case the client needs to expel or erase any of put away ID, at that point he/she have to press DEL key, subsequent to squeezing DEL key, LCD will request select area means select ID that to be erased. Presently client needs to choose ID and press OK key (same DEL key). Presently LCD will tell you that finger has erased effectively. Presently the client may check it was erased or not by setting a similar finger over the unique finger impression module and squeezing MATCH key (UP/Down key).

At the point when set finger will be legitimate Green LED will sparkle for five second and entryway additionally opens simultaneously. Following 5-seconds entryway will be shut naturally. The client may redo entryway/entryway opening and shutting as indicated by their prerequisite. Servo engine is answerable for open and shutting of the door.

Circuit Explanation:

The circuit of this Arduino Fingerprint Security System is straightforward which contains Arduino which controls entire the procedure of the task, push catch, bell, and LCD. Arduino controls the total procedures.

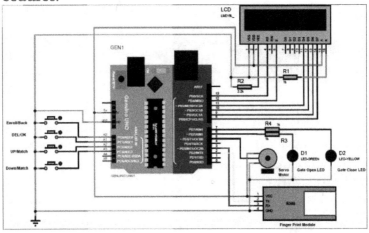

The push catch is legitimately associated with stick D14(ENROL),D15(DEL), D16(UP) and D17(DOWN) of Arduino regarding ground And Yellow LED is associated at Digital stick D7 of Arduino concerning ground through a 1k resistor and Green LED is associated with D6 of Arduino with a similar strategy. Unique finger impression Module's Rx and Tx legitimately associated at Software Serial or Digital stick D2 and D3 of Arduino. 5v supply is utilized for controlling unique mark module taken from Arduino board and Servo engine is likewise associated with PWM stick D5 of Arduino. A 16x2 LCD is arranged in 4-piece mode and its RS, EN, D4, D5, D6, and D7 are legitimately associated at Digital stick D13, D12, D11, D10, D9, and D8 of Arduino.

Note: here D14, D15, D16, D17 are A0, A1, A2, A3 separately.

Program Explanation:

In a program, we have utilized Adafruit Fingerprint Sensor Library for interfacing unique mark module with Arduino board. You can check the total Code underneath, it very well may be effectively comprehended. Here we are clarifying primary elements of the Arduino Program.

Beneath bit of code is utilized to take Finger Print as information and make a move as per approval of finger. On the off chance that finger will be approved entryway will be open generally stay shut.

```
for(int i=0;i<5;i++)

{

  lcd.clear();

  lcd.print("Place Finger");

  delay(2000);

  int result=getFingerprintIDez();

  if(result>=0)

  {

    digitalWrite(openLight, HIGH);

    digitalWrite(closeLight, LOW);

    lcd.clear();
```

```
lcd.print("Allowed");

lcd.setCursor(0,1);

lcd.print("Gete Opened  ");

myServo.write(0);

delay(5000);

myServo.write(180);

digitalWrite(closeLight, HIGH);

digitalWrite(openLight, LOW);

lcd.setCursor(0,1);

lcd.print("Gate Closed  ");
```

Given void checkKeys() work is utilized for checking Enroll or DEL key is squeezed or not and what to do whenever squeezed. On the off chance that the Enroll key squeezed the Enroll() work is called and DEL key press at that point erase() work is called.

```
void checkKeys()

{
```

```
if(digitalRead(enroll) == 0)

{

lcd.clear();

lcd.print("Please Wait");

delay(1000);

while(digitalRead(enroll) == 0);

Enroll();

}

else if(digitalRead(del) == 0)

{

lcd.clear();

lcd.print("Please Wait");

delay(1000);

delet();

}
```

```
}
```

Given capacity is utilized for entering ID to be erased and calling uint8_t deleteFingerprint(uint8_t id) work that will erase finger from records.

```
void delet()

{

  int count=0;

  lcd.clear();

  lcd.print("Delete Finger  ");

  lcd.setCursor(0,1);

  lcd.print("Location:");

  while(1)

  {

   lcd.setCursor(9,1);

   lcd.print(count);

   if(digitalRead(up) == 0)
```

```
{

  count++;

  if(count>25)

  count=0;

  delay(500);

  }

.... .....

..... .....
```

Given capacity is utilized for erase unique mark from the record of chosen ID.

```
uint8_t deleteFingerprint(uint8_t id)

{

  uint8_t p = -1;

  lcd.clear();

  lcd.print("Please wait");
```

```
p = finger.deleteModel(id);

if(p == FINGERPRINT_OK)

{

  Serial.println("Deleted!");

  lcd.clear();

  lcd.print("Figer Deleted");

  lcd.setCursor(0,1);

  lcd.print("Successfully");

  delay(1000);

}

else

{

  Serial.print("Something Wrong");

  lcd.clear();

  lcd.print("Something Wrong");
```

```
lcd.setCursor(0,1);

lcd.print("Try Again Later");

delay(2000);

return p;

}

}
```

Given Function is accustomed to taking unique mark picture and convert them into the layout and spare it by chose ID into the unique finger impression module memory.

```
uint8_t getFingerprintEnroll()

{

int p = -1;

lcd.clear();

lcd.print("finger ID:");

lcd.print(id);
```

```
lcd.setCursor(0,1);

lcd.print("Place Finger");

delay(2000);

while (p != FINGERPRINT_OK)

{

 p = finger.getImage();

..... .....

....... ....
```

So that is the way we can utilize Arduino with Finger Print Reader Module for Security System.

Code

```
#include<LiquidCrystal.h>
LiquidCrystal lcd(13,12,11,10,9,8);
#include <SoftwareSerial.h>
SoftwareSerial fingerPrint(2, 3);
#include<Servo.h>
Servo myServo;
#include <Adafruit_Fingerprint.h>
uint8_t id;
Adafruit_Fingerprint   finger   =   Adafruit_Finger-
```

```
print(&fingerPrint);
#define enroll 14
#define del 15
#define up 16
#define down 17
#define openLight 6
#define closeLight 7
#define servoPin 5
void setup()
{
  delay(1000);
  myServo.attach(servoPin);
  myServo.write(180);
  pinMode(enroll, INPUT_PULLUP);
  pinMode(up, INPUT_PULLUP);
  pinMode(down, INPUT_PULLUP);
  pinMode(del, INPUT_PULLUP);
  pinMode(openLight, OUTPUT);
  pinMode(closeLight, OUTPUT);
  lcd.begin(16,2);
  lcd.print("Security System");
  lcd.setCursor(0,1);
  lcd.print("by Finger Print");
  delay(2000);
  lcd.clear();
  lcd.print("Hello World");
  lcd.setCursor(0,1);
  lcd.print("Saddam Khan");
  delay(2000);
  finger.begin(57600);
```

```
Serial.begin(9600);
lcd.clear();
lcd.print("Finding Module");
lcd.setCursor(0,1);
delay(1000);
if (finger.verifyPassword())
{
 Serial.println("Found fingerprint sensor!");
 lcd.clear();
 lcd.print("Found Module ");
 delay(1000);
}
else
{
Serial.println("Did not find fingerprint sensor :(");
lcd.clear();
lcd.print("module not Found");
lcd.setCursor(0,1);
lcd.print("Check Connections");
while (1);
}
}
void loop()
{
lcd.setCursor(0,0);
lcd.print("Press UP/Down ");
lcd.setCursor(0,1);
lcd.print("to start System");
digitalWrite(closeLight, HIGH);
if(digitalRead(up)==0 || digitalRead(down)==0)
```

```
{
 for(int i=0;i<5;i++)
 {
 lcd.clear();
 lcd.print("Place Finger");
 delay(2000);
 int result=getFingerprintIDez();
 if(result>=0)
 {
   digitalWrite(openLight, HIGH);
   digitalWrite(closeLight, LOW);
   lcd.clear();
   lcd.print("Allowed");
   lcd.setCursor(0,1);
   lcd.print("Gete Opened ");
   myServo.write(0);
   delay(5000);
   myServo.write(180);
   digitalWrite(closeLight, HIGH);
   digitalWrite(openLight, LOW);
   lcd.setCursor(0,1);
   lcd.print("Gate Closed ");
   return;
  }
 }
}
checkKeys();
delay(1000);
}
void checkKeys()
```

```
{
 if(digitalRead(enroll) == 0)
 {
 lcd.clear();
 lcd.print("Please Wait");
 delay(1000);
 while(digitalRead(enroll) == 0);
 Enroll();
 }
 else if(digitalRead(del) == 0)
 {
 lcd.clear();
 lcd.print("Please Wait");
 delay(1000);
 delet();
 }
}
void Enroll()
{
 int count=0;
 lcd.clear();
 lcd.print("Enroll Finger  ");
 lcd.setCursor(0,1);
 lcd.print("Location:");
 while(1)
 {
 lcd.setCursor(9,1);
 lcd.print(count);
 if(digitalRead(up) == 0)
 {
```

```
  count++;
  if(count>25)
  count=0;
  delay(500);
  }
 else if(digitalRead(down) == 0)
 {
  count--;
  if(count<0)
  count=25;
  delay(500);
 }
 else if(digitalRead(del) == 0)
 {
   id=count;
   getFingerprintEnroll();
   return;
 }
  else if(digitalRead(enroll) == 0)
  {
    return;
  }
}
}
void delet()
{
 int count=0;
 lcd.clear();
 lcd.print("Delete Finger  ");
 lcd.setCursor(0,1);
```

```
lcd.print("Location:");
while(1)
{
 lcd.setCursor(9,1);
 lcd.print(count);
 if(digitalRead(up) == 0)
 {
  count++;
  if(count>25)
  count=0;
  delay(500);
 }
 else if(digitalRead(down) == 0)
 {
  count--;
  if(count<0)
  count=25;
  delay(500);
 }
 else if(digitalRead(del) == 0)
 {
   id=count;
   deleteFingerprint(id);
   return;
 }
  else if(digitalRead(enroll) == 0)
 {
   return;
 }
}
```

```
}
uint8_t getFingerprintEnroll()
{
 int p = -1;
 lcd.clear();
 lcd.print("finger ID:");
 lcd.print(id);
 lcd.setCursor(0,1);
 lcd.print("Place Finger");
 delay(2000);
 while (p != FINGERPRINT_OK)
 {
  p = finger.getImage();
  switch (p)
  {
  case FINGERPRINT_OK:
   Serial.println("Image taken");
   lcd.clear();
   lcd.print("Image taken");
   break;
  case FINGERPRINT_NOFINGER:
   Serial.println("No Finger");
   lcd.clear();
   lcd.print("No Finger");
   break;
  case FINGERPRINT_PACKETRECIEVEERR:
   Serial.println("Communication error");
   lcd.clear();
   lcd.print("Comm Error");
   break;
```

```
case FINGERPRINT_IMAGEFAIL:
 Serial.println("Imaging error");
 lcd.clear();
 lcd.print("Imaging Error");
 break;
default:
 Serial.println("Unknown error");
 lcd.clear();
 lcd.print("Unknown Error");
 break;
}
}
// OK success!
p = finger.image2Tz(1);
switch (p) {
 case FINGERPRINT_OK:
  Serial.println("Image converted");
  lcd.clear();
  lcd.print("Image converted");
  break;
 case FINGERPRINT_IMAGEMESS:
  Serial.println("Image too messy");
  lcd.clear();
  lcd.print("Image too messy");
  return p;
 case FINGERPRINT_PACKETRECIEVEERR:
  Serial.println("Communication error");
  lcd.clear();
  lcd.print("Comm Error");
  return p;
```

```
 case FINGERPRINT_FEATUREFAIL:
  Serial.println("Could not find fingerprint features");
  lcd.clear();
  lcd.print("Feature Not Found");
  return p;
 case FINGERPRINT_INVALIDIMAGE:
  Serial.println("Could not find fingerprint features");
  lcd.clear();
  lcd.print("Feature Not Found");
  return p;
 default:
  Serial.println("Unknown error");
  lcd.clear();
  lcd.print("Unknown Error");
  return p;
}


 Serial.println("Remove finger");
lcd.clear();
lcd.print("Remove Finger");
delay(2000);
p = 0;
while (p != FINGERPRINT_NOFINGER) {
 p = finger.getImage();
}
Serial.print("ID "); Serial.println(id);
p = -1;
Serial.println("Place same finger again");
 lcd.clear();
  lcd.print("Place Finger");
```

```
  lcd.setCursor(0,1);
  lcd.print("  Again");
 while (p != FINGERPRINT_OK) {
  p = finger.getImage();
  switch (p) {
  case FINGERPRINT_OK:
   Serial.println("Image taken");
   break;
  case FINGERPRINT_NOFINGER:
   Serial.print(".");
   break;
  case FINGERPRINT_PACKETRECIEVEERR:
   Serial.println("Communication error");
   break;
  case FINGERPRINT_IMAGEFAIL:
   Serial.println("Imaging error");
   break;
  default:
   Serial.println("Unknown error");
   return;
  }
 }
 // OK success!
 p = finger.image2Tz(2);
 switch (p) {
  case FINGERPRINT_OK:
   Serial.println("Image converted");
   break;
  case FINGERPRINT_IMAGEMESS:
   Serial.println("Image too messy");
```

```
  return p;
 case FINGERPRINT_PACKETRECIEVEERR:
  Serial.println("Communication error");
  return p;
 case FINGERPRINT_FEATUREFAIL:
  Serial.println("Could not find fingerprint features");
  return p;
 case FINGERPRINT_INVALIDIMAGE:
  Serial.println("Could not find fingerprint features");
  return p;
 default:
  Serial.println("Unknown error");
  return p;
}


 // OK converted!
 Serial.print("Creating model for #");  Serial.println(id);


 p = finger.createModel();
 if (p == FINGERPRINT_OK) {
 Serial.println("Prints matched!");
 } else if (p == FINGERPRINT_PACKETRECIEVEERR) {
 Serial.println("Communication error");
  return p;
 } else if (p == FINGERPRINT_ENROLLMISMATCH) {
 Serial.println("Fingerprints did not match");
  return p;
 } else {
```

```
  Serial.println("Unknown error");
  return p;
 }


  Serial.print("ID "); Serial.println(id);
  p = finger.storeModel(id);
  if (p == FINGERPRINT_OK) {
   Serial.println("Stored!");
   lcd.clear();
   lcd.print("Stored!");
   delay(2000);
  } else if (p == FINGERPRINT_PACKETRECIEVEERR) {
   Serial.println("Communication error");
   return p;
  } else if (p == FINGERPRINT_BADLOCATION) {
   Serial.println("Could not store in that location");
   return p;
  } else if (p == FINGERPRINT_FLASHERR) {
   Serial.println("Error writing to flash");
   return p;
  }
  else {
   Serial.println("Unknown error");
   return p;
  }
 }
int getFingerprintIDez()
{
 uint8_t p = finger.getImage();
```

```
 if(p != FINGERPRINT_OK)
return -1;

p = finger.image2Tz();
if(p != FINGERPRINT_OK)
return -1;

p = finger.fingerFastSearch();
if(p != FINGERPRINT_OK)
{
lcd.clear();
lcd.print("Finger Not Found");
lcd.setCursor(0,1);
lcd.print("Try Later");
delay(2000);
return -1;
}
// found a match!
Serial.print("Found ID #");
Serial.print(finger.fingerID);
return finger.fingerID;
}
uint8_t deleteFingerprint(uint8_t id)
{
uint8_t p = -1;
lcd.clear();
lcd.print("Please wait");
p = finger.deleteModel(id);
if(p == FINGERPRINT_OK)
{
  Serial.println("Deleted!");
```

```
lcd.clear();
lcd.print("Figer Deleted");
lcd.setCursor(0,1);
lcd.print("Successfully");
delay(1000);
}


else
{
Serial.print("Something Wrong");
lcd.clear();
lcd.print("Something Wrong");
lcd.setCursor(0,1);
lcd.print("Try Again Later");
delay(2000);
return p;
}
}
```

6. BRILLIANT KNOCK DETECTING DOOR LOCK UTILIZING ARDUINO

Security is a significant worry in our everyday life, and advanced locks have turned into a significant piece of these security frameworks. There are numerous kinds of security frameworks accessible to verify our place. A few models are PIR based Security System, RFID based Security System, Digital Lock System, bio-framework frameworks, Electronics Code lock. In this post, let us construct a Secret Knock Detecting Door Lock utilizing Arduino which can distinguish the example of your thumps at the entry way and will possibly open the lock if the thumping example matches with the right example.

Components:

- Arduino Uno
- Buzzer
- Push Button
- Power
- 1M Resistor
- Box
- Connecting wires
- Servo Motor

Circuit Explanation:

The circuit Diagram of this Knocking Pattern Detector is extremely straightforward which contains Arduino for controlling entire the procedure of the venture, push catch, ringer, and Servo Motor. Arduino controls the total procedures like taking secret word structure Buzzer or Sensor, contrasting examples, driving Servo for open and close the entryway and spare the example to Arduino.

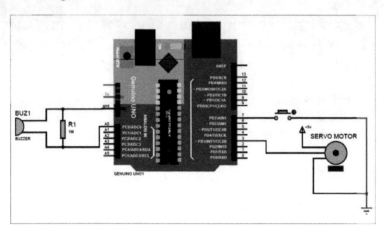

The push catch is legitimately associated with stick D7 of Arduino regarding ground. What's more, a ringer is associated at simple stick A0 of Arduino as for ground and with a 1M opposition among A0 and ground moreover. A Servo engine is additionally associated with PWM stick D3 of Arduino.

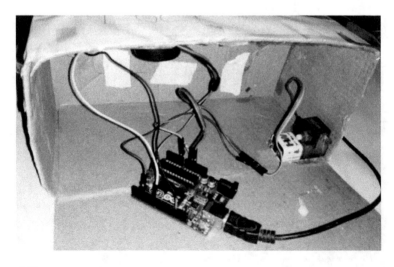

Feeding Knocking Pattern in Arduino:

In this circuit, we have utilized Buzzer or Peizo Sensor to take thump information design in the framework. Here we are utilizing a push catch to permit to take contribution from the sensor and furthermore spare that into the Arduino. This framework is planned by taking thought from Morse code design however not actually comparable with that.

Here we have utilized a card board box for exhibition. To take input we thump over the board in the wake of squeezing push button. Here we have thumped by remembering a timespan that is 500ms. This 500ms is on the grounds that we have fixed it in code and info example is relying on it. This 500ms timespan will characterize the info was 1 or 0. Check the code underneath to comprehend this thing.

At the point when we thump it, Arduino starts observing the hour of the primary thump to second thump and place that in a cluster. Here in this framework, we are taking 6 thumps. It implies we will get 5 timeframes.

Presently we check the timeframe individually. To start with, we check timespan between first thump and second thump in the event that the time contrast between these less the 500ms, at that point it will be 0 and if more noteworthy than 500ms it will be 1 and it will be spared into a variable. Presently after it, we check timeframe between second thump and third thump, etc.

At long last, we will get 5 digit yield in 0 and 1 organization (double).

Working Explanation:

Working of Knock based Smart Lock Project is straightforward. First we need to spare an example in the framework. So we need to press and hold push button until we thump multiple times. Here in this task, I have utilized 6 thumps yet the client may transform it as they need. After multiple times thump, Arduino discover the thump example and spare that in EEPROM. Presently subsequent to sparing the info example, press and promptly discharged the drive button for taking contribution from the sensor to Arduino to open the lock. Presently we need to thump multiple times. After it, Arduino translates it and contrasts and spared design. On the off chance that a match happens, at that point Arduino open the door by driving servo engine.

Note: when we press or press and hold the push button Arduino start a 10 seconds clock to take every one of the 6 thump. Means client need to thump inside this 10 seconds time. Furthermore, the client may open Serial screen to see the log.

Programming Explanation:

In a program as a matter of first importance we incorporate the header record and characterizes information and yield stick and characterize the large scale and proclaimed factors as should be obvious in the Full Code in code segment underneath.

After this, in arrangement work, we provide guidance to characterized stick and start servo engine.

```
void setup()

{

  pinMode(sw, INPUT_PULLUP);

  myServo.attach(servoPin);

  myServo.write(180);

  Serial.begin(9600);

}
```

After it, we take information and spare the information example or thump time in an exhibit.

```
void loop()

{

  int i=0;

  if(digitalRead(sw) == LOW)

  {

    Serial.println("Start");

    delay(1000);

    long stt= millis();

    while(millis()<(stt+patternInputTime))

    {

      int temp=analogRead(A0);

      if(temp>sensitivity    &&    flag==0    &&
i<=patternLenth)

      {
```

..... .

....

After it, we translate the information design

```
for(int i=0;i<patternLenth;i++)

   {

     knok=1;

     if(slot[i+1]-slot[i]<500)

        pattern[i]=0;

     else

        pattern[i]=1;

     Serial.println(pattern[i]);

   }
```

And after that spare if push catch is as yet squeezed

```
if(digitalRead(sw)==0)
```

```
{

  for(int i=0;i<patternLenth;i++)

    EEPROM.write(i,pattern[i]);

  while(digitalRead(sw) == 0);

}
```

Furthermore, in the event that push catch isn't at present squeezed, at that point Arduino will contrast info decoded example and spared design.

```
else

  {

    if(knok == 1)

    {

      for(int i=0;i<patternLenth;i++)

      {

        if(pattern[i] == EEPROM.read(i))

        {
```

```
        Serial.println(acceptFlag++);

   }

   else

   {

     Serial.println("Break");

          break;

   }

  }

 }
```

In the event that any secret word coordinated, at that point Servo open the door generally nothing occurred except for the client may see result over sequential screen.

```
Serial.println(acceptFlag);

    if(acceptFlag >= patternLenth-1)

    {
```

```
        Serial.println(" Accepted");

        myServo.write(openGate);

        delay(5000);

        myServo.write(closeGate);

    }

    else

        Serial.println("Rejected");

}
```

You can check the total code underneath.

Code

```
#include<EEPROM.h>
#include<Servo.h>
#define patternLenth 5
#define patternInputTime 10000
#define sensitivity 80
#define margin 100
#define sw 7
#define servoPin 3
#define openGate 0
#define closeGate 180
```

```
long slot[patternLenth+1];
int pattern[patternLenth];
int flag=0;
int acceptFlag=0;
int knok;
Servo myServo;
void setup()
{
 pinMode(sw, INPUT_PULLUP);
 myServo.attach(servoPin);
 myServo.write(180);
 Serial.begin(9600);
}
void loop()
{
 int i=0;
 if(digitalRead(sw) == LOW)
 {
   Serial.println("Start");
   delay(1000);
   long stt= millis();
   while(millis()<(stt+patternInputTime))
   {
    int temp=analogRead(A0);
             if(temp>sensitivity  &&  flag==0  &&
i<=patternLenth)
    {
      delay(10);
      flag=1;
      slot[i++]=millis()-stt;
```

```
   //Serial.println(slot[i-1] - stt);
   if(i>patternLenth)
   break;
 }
 else if(temp == 0)
 flag=0;
}


   long stp=millis();
Serial.println("Stop");
// Serial.println(stp-stt);
for(int i=0;i<patternLenth;i++)
{
 knok=1;
 if(slot[i+1]-slot[i] < 500 )
  pattern[i]=0;
 else
  pattern[i]=1;
 Serial.println(pattern[i]);
}
if(digitalRead(sw) == 0)
{
 for(int i=0;i<patternLenth;i++)
  EEPROM.write(i,pattern[i]);
 while(digitalRead(sw) == 0);
}
else
{
 if(knok == 1)
```

```
{
  for(int i=0;i<patternLenth;i++)
  {
   if(pattern[i] == EEPROM.read(i))
   {
     Serial.println(acceptFlag++);
   }
   else
   {
     Serial.println("Break");
     break;
   }
  }
}
Serial.println(acceptFlag);
if(acceptFlag >= patternLenth-1)
{
  Serial.println(" Accepted");
  myServo.write(openGate);
  delay(5000);
  myServo.write(closeGate);
}
else
  Serial.println("Rejected");
}
for(int i=0;i<patternLenth;i++)
{
 pattern[i]=0;
 slot[i]=0;
}
```

```
  slot[i]=0;
  acceptFlag=0;
 }
}
```

7. CREATING TONES BY TAPPING FINGERS UTILIZING ARDUINO

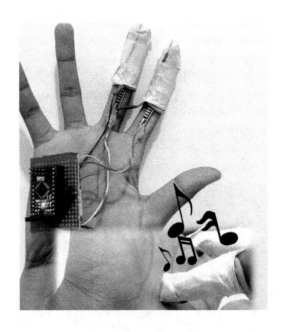

In this undertaking we are gonna to fabricate a bit of excitement utilizing Arduino. We as a whole have that propensity for tapping Table or Pen for making any arbitrary music. Obviously it probably won't be considered as a decent peculiarity, yet we as a whole appreciate doing it at any rate once. Henceforth I thought of taking it to the following level by utilizing Arduino's capacity to play tones. When you manufacture this task you would have the option to Generate tones by Tapping your fingers on anything conductive and make your very own rhythms, its like playing Piano on your palm. Sounds cool right along these lines, let us fabricate it.

Components required:

The materials required for this undertaking is recorded underneath, it isn't compulsory to adhere on to the equivalent. When you get the idea you can utilize your own particular manner of building it.

- Arduini Pro Mini
- Flex Sensor
- Peizo Speaker
- 10K Resistors
- Finger Gloves
- 9V Battery
- BC547 Transistors

Circuit Diagram and Explanation:

The circuit outline for This Arduino Palm Piano is demonstrated as follows.

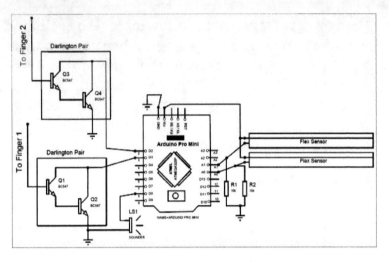

The task utilizes an aggregate of four sensor, that is two flex sensor and two Darlington sets going about as a touch sensor. We have additionally utilized two draw down resistors R1 as well as R2 of worth 10k every, which will go about as a draw down resistor for the Flex sensor. Here Flex sensor is utilized to produce Three distinct tones by utilizing one finger, in view of the amount it has bowed. So we can create 6 sounds utilizing 2 fingers. Learn here about the Flex Sensor.

Darlington Pair:

Before we continue it is essential to realize what is a Darlington and how precisely does it work in our task. Darlington pair can be characterized as two bipolar transistors associated so that the current intensified by the first is additionally enhanced continuously transistor. A Darlington pair is appeared in the picture beneath:

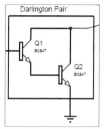

As appeared above we have utilized two BC547 transistors whose authorities are attached to assemble and the producer of the principal transistor is combined with the Base of the subsequent transistor. This circuit goes about as an intensifier with an increase, which means any little sign given to the base of the primary transistor is sufficient to predisposition the base of the subsequent transistor. Our body goes about as a ground here so at whatever point we contact the base of the transistor the subsequent transistor gets one-sided. Utilizing this to our support we have fabricated the touch sensor for this task.

Stick number 2 and 3 are the interfere with pins on the Arduino which will be pulled high utilizing inward draw up resistors and afterward these pins will be held to ground at whatever point the Darlington switch closes. Thusly each time we contact the wire (from the base of first transistor) a hinder will be activated from the Arduino.

Utilizing two fingers can deliver just two sorts of

tones thus I have additionally included a flex sensor which will adjust the tone dependent on the amount it is twisted. I have modified to deliver three unique tones for every finger dependent on how much the finger (flex sensor) is twisted. You can build the number in case you might want to have more tones readily available.

I made the total board on a perf board with the goal that it fits effectively into my palms, yet you can utilize a breadboard too. Simply ensure your body contacts the ground of the circuit sooner or later. When you weld all that it should look something like this

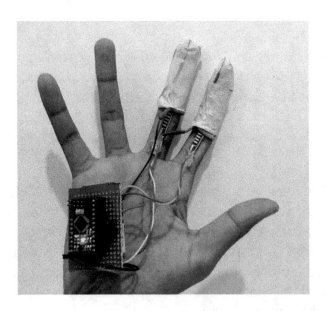

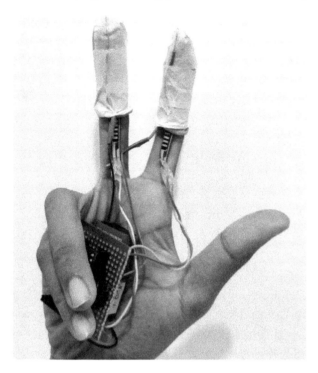

I have utilized two finger gloves to verify the wires from Darlington pair and the flex sensor in position as appeared previously. You can think of your own (better if conceivable) plan to verify them set up while you are playing your tones.

Arduino Programming:

The program for this Arduino Tap Tone Generator is quite straight forward. We simply need to pay special mind to hinders from the Darlington wires and whenever discovered one we need to play tone which relies upon how a lot of flex sensor is twisted. The total code is given toward the finish of this post yet I have clarified couple of significant pieces underneath.

Note: This program works with assistance of library "pitches.h". So ensure you have added the header document to your program before you order it. You can download the pitches.h header document from here.

In the arrangement work, we introduce stick 2 as well as 3 as Input with pull-up resistors. We additionally pronounce them as interfere with pins and execute the tone1() when there is a hinder on stick 2 and the tone2() work when there is a hinder on the third stick. These hinders will be activated at whatever point these pins get LOW from their pulled-up state.

```
void setup() {

pinMode(2, INPUT_PULLUP);

pinMode(3, INPUT_PULLUP);

attachInterrupt(digitalPinToInterrupt(2), tone1, LOW);

attachInterrupt(digitalPinToInterrupt(3), tone2, LOW);
```

```
Serial.begin(9600);

}
```

Inside the circle work, we continually check how a lot of the flex sensor is bowed. My FlexSensor 1 for instance gave values around 200 when left level and went down right to 130 when I twisted it to its most extreme, so I have mapped the incentive from 200 to 130 as 1 to 3 since I need to play 3 distinct kinds of tones. You need to change these two lines dependent on your Flex sensor esteems and number of tones.

```
void loop() {

flexSensor1 = map(analo-
gRead(A0),200,130,1,3); //Map up with your own
values based on your flex sensor

flexSensor2 = map(analo-
gRead(A1),170,185,1,3); //Map up with your own
values based on your flex sensor

}
```

As we saw before the capacity tone1() will be executed when a hinder is recognized on stick 2. What occurs inside the tone1() work is appeared previously. We take a gander at the estimations of Flex-

Sensor1 and play a tone dependent on the flexSesnor Value. Tones will be played utilizing Arduino's Tone work. We have clarified the tone() work in our past undertaking.

```
void tone1()

{

if(flexSensor1==1)

tone(8, NOTE_D4,50);

else if(flexSensor1==2)

tone(8, NOTE_A3,50);

else if(flexSensor1==3)

tone(8, NOTE_G4,50);

else

tone(8, NOTE_D4,50);

}
```

The underneath line is utilized to play the tone. You can play any tone that is accessible in the "pitches.h" header document. The above line for example plays the NOTE_A3 on stick for span of 50 milli seconds.

```
tone(8, NOTE_A3,50); //tone(PinNum,Note name, Duration);
```

Working:

When your equipment is prepared, transfer the code and mount them on your fingers. Ensure your body is contacting the ground of the circuit sooner or later. Presently essentially contact any conductive material or your body and you ought to have the option to hear the individual tone. You can play your very own tune or music by tapping at various interims and various positions.

Expectation you delighted in building the task. Additionally check our Arduino Audio Player as well as Arduino Tone Generator Project.

Cheerful tapping!!

Code

```
/*
* Arduino based Tap and Tone player
*
* ###CONNECTIONS###
* Darlington Wire 1 -> Pin 2
* Darlington Wire 2 -> Pin 3
```

```
* FlexSensor 1 -> A0
* FlexSensor 2 -> A1
* Speaker -> Pin 8
*/
#include "pitches.h"    //add this librarey into the pro-
ject folder
int flexSensor1,flexSensor2;

void setup() {
pinMode(2, INPUT_PULLUP);
pinMode(3, INPUT_PULLUP);
attachInterrupt(digitalPinToInterrupt(2),      tone1,
LOW); //Trigger tone1 when LOW
attachInterrupt(digitalPinToInterrupt(3),      tone2,
LOW); //Trigger tone2 when LOW
Serial.begin(9600);
}

void loop() {
 flexSensor1 = map(analogRead(A0),200,130,1,3); //
Map up with your own values based on your flex sen-
sor
 flexSensor2 = map(analogRead(A1),170,185,1,3); //
Map up with your own values based on your flex sen-
sor
}

//**Function to execute on Interrupt 1**//
void tone1()
{
if(flexSensor1==1)
tone(8, NOTE_D4,50);
else if(flexSensor1==2)
```

```
tone(8, NOTE_A3,50);
else if (flexSensor1 == 3)
tone(8, NOTE_G4,50);
else
tone(8, NOTE_D4,50);
}
//**Function to execute on Interrupt 2**//
void tone2()
{
if (flexSensor1 == 1)
tone(8, NOTE_A4,50);
else if (flexSensor1 == 2)
tone(8, NOTE_F4,50);
else if (flexSensor1 == 3)
tone(8, NOTE_E4,50);
else
 tone(8, NOTE_A4,50);
}
```

8. ARDUINO DATA LOGGER (LOG TEMPERATURE, HUMIDITY, TIME ON SD CARD AND COMPUTER)

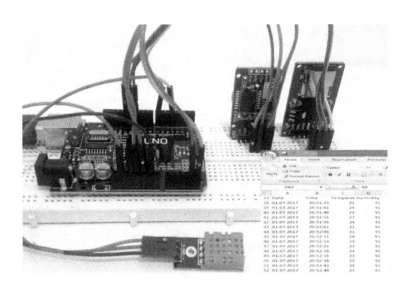

As Engineers/Developers we generally depend upon the information gathered to plan or improve a framework. Recording information and examining them is a typical practice in the vast majority of the ventures, here we are building Arduino Data Logger Project where we will figure out how we can log information at a particular interim of time. We will utilize an Arduino load up to peruse a few information (here temperature, moistness, date and time) and spare them on a SD card and the PC at the same time.

The information spared can be effectively opened in an Excel Sheet for further examinations. To keep up the date and time we will utilize the well known RTC module DS3231 and to get the Temperature and Humidity we will utilize the DHT11 Sensor. Toward the finish of the venture you will learn

- Step wise instructions to log information into SD card with Date, Time and sensor esteems.

- The most effective method to compose information legitimately to Excel Sheet on PC through sequential correspondence.

Materials Required:

- Breadboard
- Arduino UNO (any Arduino board)
- DHT11 Temperature sensor
- DS3231 RTC module
- SD card module
- SD card
- Connecting wires
- Computer/Laptop

DHT11 Temperature and Humidity Sensor

Circuit Diagram:

The circuit Diagram for this Arduino Temperature Logger Project is demonstrated as follows.

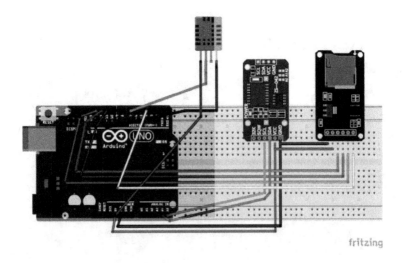

As appeared in the circuit chart the associations are

extremely basic since we have utilized them as modules we can legitimately assemble them on a breadboard. The associations are additionally ordered in the table underneath

Arduino Pin	Module Pin
Temperature Sensor – DHT11	
Vcc	5V
Gnd	Gnd
Nc	Nc
Out	Pin 7
RTC module DS3231	
Vcc	5V
Gnd	Gnd
SCL	Pin A5
SDA	Pin A4
SD card Module	
Vcc	5V
Gnd	Gnd
MISO	Pin 12
MOSI	Pin 11
SCK	Pin 13
CS	Pin 4

You can supplant the DHT11 temperature sensor with any of your sensor from which you have to log the qualities. You can check LM35 with Arduino to understand temperature.

The RTC module DS3231 is interfaced with Arduino utilizing the I2C correspondence (SCL, SDA) and the SD card module is interfaced utilizing the SPI Communication (MISO, MOSI, SCK, CS). The pins 4 and 7 are characterized as the CS stick and yield stick by Arduino program, you can transform them to some other stick whenever required. We beforehand interfaced SD card with Arduino in Music player venture.

Arduino Program Explanation:

We need to compose the Arduino program which can do the accompanying.

- Peruse information from DTH11 Sensor (or whatever other information that you wish to log).

- Instate the I2C transport to peruse information from RTC module.

- Store the Date, Time, Temperature as well as Humidity into the SD card.

- Instate the SPI transport to interface the SD

card module with Arduino.

- Store the Date, Time, Temperature as well as Humidity on an Excel Sheet running on a PC/ Laptop.

The above advances may sound muddled however they are extremely simple since we have the libraries to do the difficult activity for us. You need to download the accompanying two libraries

- DHT11 Sensor Library from GitHub

- DS3231 RTC module library from Rinky-Dink Electronics

When you have downloaded the library add them to your Arduino IDE by following

Sketch->Include Library -> Add .ZIP Library

To bolster the information from Arduino vivacious into an Excel sheet on PC we will likewise need to introduce programming called PLX-DAQ gave by Parallax Inc. Pursue the connection to download the record and introduce them dependent on your working framework. This ought to have made an organizer named PLS-DAQ on your work area. We will deal with it later in our working segment.

Presently in the wake of including the two libraries

and in the wake of introducing the product, you can utilize the Complete Code (given at base of instructional exercise) as well as transfer them to your Arduino. I have attempted my best to keep the code as straightforward as could be expected under the circumstances and the clarifications are likewise given through remark segments. Further, I will clarify the significant sections beneath.

1. Perusing Data from DS3231:

DS3231 is a RTC module. It is utilized to keep up the date and time for a large portion of the Electronics ventures. This module has its own coin cell power supply utilizing which it keeps up the date and time in any event, when the fundamental power is evacuated or the MCU has gone however a hard reset. So once we set the date as well as time in this module it will monitor it generally.

Utilizing this module is simple due to the library gave by Arduino.

```
// Init the DS3231 using the hardware interface

DS3231 rtc(SDA, SCL);

void Initialize_RTC()

{
```

```
// Initialize the rtc object

rtc.begin();

//#### the following lines can be uncommented to
set the date and time for the first time###

/*

rtc.setDOW(FRIDAY);   // Set Day-of-Week to SUN-
DAY

rtc.setTime(18, 46, 45);      // Set the time to
12:00:00 (24hr format)

rtc.setDate(6, 30, 2017);  // Set the date to January
1st, 2014

*/

}
```

Note: When utilizing this module just because you need to set the date and time. It tends to be finished by basically expelling the remarks as referenced above and composing the date and time. Ensure you remark them back and transfer it, else each time you run the load up the date and time will be set once more. You can likewise utilize RTC IC DS1307 for perusing the time with Arduino.

2. Perusing Data from DHT11:

DHT11 is a Temperature come Humidity sensor. It sends the estimations of temperature and mugginess as a 8-piece information sequentially through the yield stick of the module. The library peruses this information by utilizing the product sequential capacity of the Arduino.

```
#define DHT11_PIN 7 //Sensor output pin is connected to pin 7

dht DHT; //Sensor object named as DHT

void Read_DHT11()

{

int chk = DHT.read11(DHT11_PIN);

}
```

Here I have associated the yield stick to stick 7 as model you can pick any stick that supports Software Serial. Calling DHT.read(pin number); will peruse the estimation of temperature and moistness and store it in the parameter DHT.temperature and DHT.Humidity separately. Likewise check this DHT11 based Arduino Temperature Measurement.

3. Introducing the SC card module:

```
void Initialize_SDcard()

{

  // see if the card is present and can be initialized:

  if (!SD.begin(chipSelect)) {

    Serial.println("Card failed, or not present");

    // don't do anything more:

    return;

  }

  // open the file. note that only one file can be open
at a time,

  // so you have to close this one before opening
another.

  File dataFile = SD.open("LoggerCD.txt", FILE_
WRITE);

  // if the file is available, write to it:
```

```
if(dataFile){

  dataFile.println("Date,Time,Temperature,Humid-
ity"); //Write the first row of the excel file

  dataFile.close();

}

}
```

Utilizing a SD card with Arduino is simple as a result of the SD card library which will be added to the Arduino IDE of course. In the SD card instate work we will make a book record named "LoggerCD.txt" and compose the primary line of our substance. Here we separate the qualities by utilizing a "," as a delimiter. Which means when a comma is put it implies we need to move to the following cell in the Excel sheet.

4. Composing Data to SD card

```
void Write_SDcard()

{

  // open the file. note that only one file can be
open at a time,
```

```
// so you have to close this one before opening
another.

File dataFile = SD.open("LoggerCD.txt", FILE_
WRITE);

// if the file is available, write to it:

if (dataFile) {

    dataFile.print(rtc.getDateStr()); //Store date on
SD card

    dataFile.print(","); //Move to next column using
a ","

    dataFile.print(rtc.getTimeStr()); //Store date on
SD card

    dataFile.print(","); //Move to next column using
a ","

    dataFile.print(DHT.temperature); //Store date
on SD card

    dataFile.print(","); //Move to next column using
a ","

    dataFile.print(DHT.humidity); //Store date on
SD card
```

```
   dataFile.print(","); //Move to next column using
a","

   dataFile.println(); //End of Row move to next
row

   dataFile.close(); //Close the file

}

else

Serial.println("OOPS!! SD card writing failed");

}
```

As said before we will probably spare the Date, Time, Temperature and Humidity into our SD card. With the assistance of the DS3231 library and the DHT11 library our Arduino will be fit for perusing all these four parameters and putting away them into the accompanying parameters as appeared in table beneath

Date	rtc.getDateStr());
Time	rtc.getTimeStr());
Temperature	DHT.temperature
Humidity	DHT.humidity

Presently we can straightforwardly utilize these parameters to store them on the SD card utilizing the print line

dataFile.print(parameter);

You can see that every parameter is isolated by a comma to make it look readable and a dataFile.println(); is utilized to demonstrate the stopping point.

5. Composing Data to PLX-DAQ

PLX-DAQ is Microsoft Excel Plug-in programming that causes us to compose esteems from Arduino to straightforwardly into an Excel record on our Laptop or PC. This is my undisputed top choice as a result of two reasons:

1.You can compose and screen the information simultaneously and gives us approach to plot them as diagrams.

2. You needn't bother with a RTC Module like DS3231 to monitor date and time. You can essentially utilize the date and time running on your Laptop/PC and spare them legitimately on Excel.

To utilize this product with Arduino we need to

send the information sequentially in a particular example simply like showing an incentive on sequential screen. The key lines are clarified beneath:

```
void Initialize_PlxDaq()

{

Serial.println("CLEARDATA"); //clears up any data left from previous projects

Serial.println("LABEL,Date,Time,Temperature,Humidity"); //always write LABEL, to indicate it as first line

}

void Write_PlxDaq()

  {

   Serial.print("DATA"); //always write "DATA" to Inidicate the following as Data

   Serial.print(","); //Move to next column using a ","

   Serial.print("DATE"); //Store date on Excel

   Serial.print(","); //Move to next column using a ","
```

```
    Serial.print("TIME"); //Store date on Excel

    Serial.print(","); //Move to next column using a ","

    Serial.print(DHT.temperature); //Store date on
Excel

    Serial.print(","); //Move to next column using a ","

    Serial.print(DHT.humidity); //Store date on
Excel

    Serial.print(","); //Move to next column using a ","

    Serial.println(); //End of Row move to next row

}
```

The product can perceive catchphrases like LABEL, DATA, TIME, DATE and so forth. As appeared in the Initialize work the catchphrase "Name" is utilized to compose the principal ROW of the Excel sheet. Later in the Write work we utilize the catchphrase "Information" to demonstrate that the accompanying data ought to be considered as DATA. To demonstrate that we need to move to next line we need to utilize comma (","). To show the finish of line we need to send a Serial.println();.

As said before we can compose the framework date

and time by sending the catchphrases "DATE" and "TIME" individually as appeared previously.

Note: Do not utilize sequential screen when utilizing this PLX_DAQ programming.

Working Explanation:

Working of the Arduino Data Logger is straightforward. When the equipment and the product are prepared the time has come to consume the program into your Arduino Board. As soon your program gets transferred, your temperature and moistness esteems will begin to get put away in your SD card. You need to pursue the means beneath to empower PLX-DAQ to log the into Excel sheet in the PC.

Stage 1: Open the "Plx-Daq Spreadsheet" record that was made on your work area during establishment.

Stage 2: If there is a Security square, click on Options->Enable the substance - > Finish - > OK to get the accompanying screen.

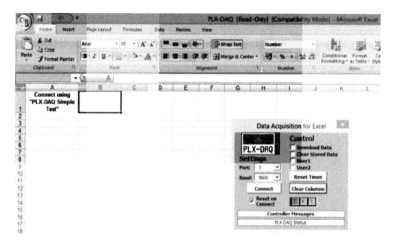

Stage 3: Now select the baud rate as "9600" and the port to which your Arduino is associated and click on Connect. Your qualities should begin to get logged like appeared in the image beneath.

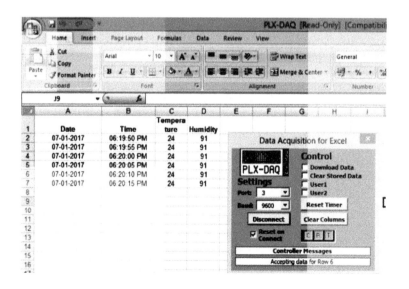

You can leave this exceed expectations sheet open and screen the qualities as they get logged. As this is occurring our SD card would likewise have spared similar qualities. To check is that is working just expel the SD card and open it on your Computer. You should discover a book document named "Logger-CD.txt" in it. At the point when opened it would look something like this.

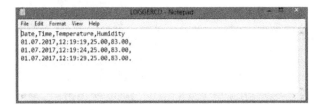

This document has information, yet it is difficult to examine them on a scratch pad. Henceforth we can open it on Excel as a CSV (Comma isolated qualities) document, consequently making it progressively viable. To open in exceed expectations

1.Open Excel. Snap on File->Open and select "All record" at base right corner and select the "LoggerCD" document from the SD card. This will open a content import wizard.

2.Click on "Next" as well as select comma as a delimiter. Snap on "Next" once more. At that point Finish.

3.Now your qualities will be opened in an Excel document as demonstrated as follows

	A	B	C	D	E	F	G	H	I
1	Date	Time	Temperat	Humidity					
2	01.07.2017	12:19:19	25	83					
3	01.07.2017	12:19:24	25	83					
4	01.07.2017	12:19:29	25	83					
5									
6									

I have logged the qualities for like clockwork; you can log them for any ideal time by changing the postpone work in the program.

Reward Improvement-Wireless Data Logging Using Arduino:

When you have prevailing so far, at that point with couple of progressions and simply including a couple of lines of code you can log information remotely.

Essentially associate a Bluetooth Device like HC-05 and compose the information to PLX-DAQ through Bluetooth rather than Serial. That is supplant Serial.print(parameter); with BluetoothName.print(parameter); as well as interface your Laptop to your Bluetooth Module a select the COM port to which your Laptops Bluetooth is associated and Taadaaa...... You have a working a Wireless Data Logging System in the blink of an eye.

Code

```
/*
 * Program to demonstrate Data Logging/Visualisa-
tion using Arduino
 *
 * ###Connection with SD card module###
 * Vcc->5V
 * Gnd->Gnd
 * MISO->pin 12
 * MOSI->pin 11
 * SCK-> pin 13
 * CS-> pin 4
 *
 * ###Connection with DS3231###
 * Vcc->5V
 * Gns->Gnd
```

```
* SCL->pin A5
* SDA-> pin A4
*
* ###Connection with DT11###
* Vcc->5V
* Gnd->Gnd
* Out-> pin 7
*
*
*/
```

#include <DS3231.h> //Library for RTC module (Download from Link in article)

#include <SPI.h> //Library for SPI communication (Pre-Loaded into Arduino)

#include <SD.h> //Library for SD card (Pre-Loaded into Arduino)

#include <dht.h> //Library for dht11 Temperature and Humidity sensor (Download from Link in article)

#define DHT11_PIN 7 //Sensor output pin is connected to pin 7

dht DHT; //Sensor object named as DHT

const int chipSelect = 4; //SD card CS pin connected to pin 4 of Arduino

// Init the DS3231 using the hardware interface

DS3231 rtc(SDA, SCL);

void setup()

{

  // Setup Serial connection

  Serial.begin(9600);

  Initialize_SDcard();

```
 Initialize_RTC();
 Initialize_PlxDaq();
}
void loop()
{
 Read_DHT11();
 Write_SDcard();
 Write_PlxDaq();
 delay(5000); //Wait for 5 seconds before writing the
next data
}
void Write_PlxDaq()
{
  Serial.print("DATA"); //always write "DATA" to Indi-
cate the following as Data
  Serial.print(","); //Move to next column using a ","
  Serial.print("DATE"); //Store date on Excel
  Serial.print(","); //Move to next column using a ","
  Serial.print("TIME"); //Store date on Excel
  Serial.print(","); //Move to next column using a ","
     Serial.print(DHT.temperature); //Store date on
Excel
  Serial.print(","); //Move to next column using a ","
  Serial.print(DHT.humidity); //Store date on Excel
  Serial.print(","); //Move to next column using a ","
  Serial.println(); //End of Row move to next row
 }
void Initialize_PlxDaq()
{
```

```
Serial.println("CLEARDATA"); //clears up any data left
from previous projects
Serial.println("LABEL,Date,Time,Temperature,Hu-
midity"); //always write LABEL, to indicate it as first
line
}
void Write_SDcard()
{
  // open the file. note that only one file can be open at
a time,
  // so you have to close this one before opening an-
other.
    File dataFile = SD.open("LoggerCD.txt", FILE_
WRITE);
 // if the file is available, write to it:
 if (dataFile) {
   dataFile.print(rtc.getDateStr()); //Store date on SD
card
  dataFile.print(","); //Move to next column using a ","
   dataFile.print(rtc.getTimeStr()); //Store date on SD
card
  dataFile.print(","); //Move to next column using a ","
  dataFile.print(DHT.temperature); //Store date on SD
card
  dataFile.print(","); //Move to next column using a ","
   dataFile.print(DHT.humidity); //Store date on SD
card
  dataFile.print(","); //Move to next column using a ","
  dataFile.println(); //End of Row move to next row
  dataFile.close(); //Close the file
```

```
}
else
Serial.println("OOPS!! SD card writing failed");
}
void Initialize_SDcard()
{
 // see if the card is present and can be initialized:
 if (!SD.begin(chipSelect)) {
   Serial.println("Card failed, or not present");
   // don't do anything more:
   return;
 }
 // open the file. note that only one file can be open at
a time,
 // so you have to close this one before opening an-
other.
    File dataFile = SD.open("LoggerCD.txt", FILE_
WRITE);
 // if the file is available, write to it:
 if (dataFile) {
    dataFile.println("Date,Time,Temperature,Humid-
ity"); //Write the first row of the excel file
   dataFile.close();
 }
}
void Initialize_RTC()
{
 // Initialize the rtc object
 rtc.begin();
//#### The following lines can be uncommented to
```

set the date and time for the first time###
```
/*
rtc.setDOW(FRIDAY);   // Set Day-of-Week to SUNDAY
rtc.setTime(18, 46, 45);   // Set the time to 12:00:00
(24hr format)
rtc.setDate(6, 30, 2017);   // Set the date to January
1st, 2014
*/
}
void Read_DHT11()
{
int chk = DHT.read11(DHT11_PIN);
}
/*void Read_DateTime()
{
 // Send date
 Serial.print(rtc.getDateStr());
 Serial.print(" -- ");
 // Send time
 Serial.println(rtc.getTimeStr());
}*/
/*void Read_TempHum()
{
 Serial.print("Temperature = ");
 Serial.println(DHT.temperature);
 Serial.print("Humidity = ");
 Serial.println(DHT.humidity);
 // delay(1000);
}*/
```

9. PLAYING MELODIES UTILIZING ARDUINO TONE() FUNCTION

Arduino is a great method to rearrange and accelerate your microcontroller ventures, on account of its locale of designers who have made nearly everything look basic. There are loads of Arduino Projects around here for you to attempt to have a ton of fun. A portion of your undertakings may require a few sounds activity to inform about something or just to intrigue the watchers. Imagine a scenario where I revealed to you that practically any signature tunes that could be played on a piano can be imitated on your Arduino with the assistance of a straightforward program and a modest Piezo speaker.

In this instructional exercise we will figure out how basic and simple it is to Play Melody on Piezo Buzzer or Speaker utilizing the Arduino tone () work. Toward the finish of this instructional exercise you will have the option to play some popular tones of Pirates of Caribbean, Crazy Frog, Super Mario and Titanic. You will likewise figure out how to play any bit of piano music with Arduino.

Hardware Required:

- Arduino (any adaptation – UNO is utilized here)

- Breadboard

- Piezo Speaker/Buzzer or some other 8ohm speaker.

- Push catches

- Interfacing Wires

- 1k resistor (discretionary)

Understanding the *Tone()* function of Arduino:

Before we can see how a tone () functions we should know how a Piezo signal functions. We may have found out about Piezo precious stones in our school, it is only a gem which changes over mechanical vibrations into power or the other way around. Here we apply a variable current (recurrence) for which the precious stone vibrates therefore creating sound. Consequently so as to make the Piezo ringer to make some clamor we need to make the Piezo electric precious stone to vibrate, the pitch and tone of commotion relies upon how quick the gem vibrates. Henceforth the tone and pitch can be constrained by shifting the recurrence of the current.

Alright, so how would we get a variable recurrence from Arduino? This is the place the tone () capacity comes in. The tone () can produce a specific recurrence on a particular stick. The time length can likewise be referenced whenever required. The grammar for tone () is

Syntax

tone(pin, frequency)

tone(pin, frequency, duration)

Parameters

pin: the pin on which to generate the tone

frequency: the frequency of the tone in hertz - unsigned int

duration: the duration of the tone in milliseconds (optional) - unsigned long

The estimations of stick can be any of your computerized stick. I have utilized stick number 8 here. The recurrence that can be created relies upon the size of the clock in your Arduino load up. For UNO and most other basic sheets the base recurrence that can be delivered is 31Hz and the greatest recurrence that can be created is 65535Hz. Anyway we people can hear just frequencies somewhere in the range of 2000Hz and 5000 Hz.

The *pitches.h* header file:

Presently, we realize how to deliver some clamor utilizing the arduino tone() work. However, how would we know what sort of tone will be produced for every recurrence?

Arduino have given us a note table which likens every recurrence to a particular melodic note type. This note table was initially composed by Brett Hagman, on whose work the tone() direction was based. We will utilize this note table to play our subjects. In case you are somebody acquainted with sheet music you ought to have the option to comprehend this table, for others like me these are simply one more square of code.

```
#define NOTE_B0 31

#define NOTE_C1 33

#define NOTE_CS1 35

#define NOTE_D1 37

#define NOTE_DS1 39

#define NOTE_E1 41

#define NOTE_F1 44

#define NOTE_FS1 46

#define NOTE_G1 49

#define NOTE_GS1 52

#define NOTE_A1 55

#define NOTE_AS1 58

#define NOTE_B1 62
```

```
#define NOTE_C2 65

#define NOTE_CS2 69

#define NOTE_D2 73

#define NOTE_DS2 78

#define NOTE_E2 82

#define NOTE_F2 87

#define NOTE_FS2 93

#define NOTE_G2 98

#define NOTE_GS2 104

#define NOTE_A2 110

#define NOTE_AS2 117

#define NOTE_B2 123

#define NOTE_C3 131

#define NOTE_CS3 139

#define NOTE_D3 147
```

```
#define NOTE_DS3 156

#define NOTE_E3 165

#define NOTE_F3 175

#define NOTE_FS3 185

#define NOTE_G3 196

#define NOTE_GS3 208

#define NOTE_A3 220

#define NOTE_AS3 233

#define NOTE_B3 247

#define NOTE_C4 262

#define NOTE_CS4 277

#define NOTE_D4 294

#define NOTE_DS4 311

#define NOTE_E4 330

#define NOTE_F4 349
```

```
#define NOTE_FS4 370

#define NOTE_G4 392

#define NOTE_GS4 415

#define NOTE_A4 440

#define NOTE_AS4 466

#define NOTE_B4 494

#define NOTE_C5 523

#define NOTE_CS5 554

#define NOTE_D5 587

#define NOTE_DS5 622

#define NOTE_E5 659

#define NOTE_F5 698

#define NOTE_FS5 740

#define NOTE_G5 784

#define NOTE_GS5 831
```

```
#define NOTE_A5 880

#define NOTE_AS5 932

#define NOTE_B5 988

#define NOTE_C6 1047

#define NOTE_CS6 1109

#define NOTE_D6 1175

#define NOTE_DS6 1245

#define NOTE_E6 1319

#define NOTE_F6 1397

#define NOTE_FS6 1480

#define NOTE_G6 1568

#define NOTE_GS6 1661

#define NOTE_A6 1760

#define NOTE_AS6 1865

#define NOTE_B6 1976
```

```
#define NOTE_C7 2093

#define NOTE_CS7 2217

#define NOTE_D7 2349

#define NOTE_DS7 2489

#define NOTE_E7 2637

#define NOTE_F7 2794

#define NOTE_FS7 2960

#define NOTE_G7 3136

#define NOTE_GS7 3322

#define NOTE_A7 3520

#define NOTE_AS7 3729

#define NOTE_B7 3951

#define NOTE_C8 4186

#define NOTE_CS8 4435

#define NOTE_D8 4699
```

```
#define NOTE_DS8 4978
```

Above code is given in pitches.h header record in this compress document, you simply need to download and incorporate this record in our Arduino code as given toward the end this instructional exercise or utilize the code given in the compress record.

Playing Musical Notes on Arduino:

To play a nice song utilizing Arduino we should realize what establishes these tunes. The three principle elements required to play a subject are

- Note esteem

- Note Duration

- Beat

We have the pitches.h header document to play any note esteem, presently we should discover its particular note span to play it. Rhythm is only how quick the tune ought to be played. When you realize the Note worth and Note term you can utilize them with the tone() like

```
tone (pinName, Note Value, Note Duration);
```

For the tones played in this instructional exercise I have given you the note Value and Note length inside the "themes.h" header document utilizing which you can play them in your undertakings. Be that as it may, on the off chance that you have a particular tone in your mine and you need to play it in your task read on.... Else skirt this theme and tumble down to the following.

To play a particular tone you need to get the sheet music of that specific music as well as convert sheet music to Arduino sketch by perusing the note worth and note length from it. In case you are a melodic understudy it would be simple for you, else invested some energy and break you head as I did. In any case, toward the day's end when your tone plays on the Piezo bell you will discover your exertion justified, despite all the trouble.

When you have the note worth and note span, load them into the program inside the "themes.h" header document as demonstrated as follows

```
//###############**"HE IS A PIRATE" Theme song
of Pirates of caribbean**##############//

int Pirates_note[] = {

NOTE_D4,   NOTE_D4,   NOTE_D4,   NOTE_D4,
NOTE_D4, NOTE_D4, NOTE_D4, NOTE_D4,
```

NOTE_D4, NOTE_D4, NOTE_D4, NOTE_D4, NOTE_D4, NOTE_D4, NOTE_D4, NOTE_D4,

NOTE_D4, NOTE_D4, NOTE_D4, NOTE_D4, NOTE_D4, NOTE_D4, NOTE_D4, NOTE_D4,

NOTE_A3, NOTE_C4, NOTE_D4, NOTE_D4, NOTE_D4, NOTE_E4, NOTE_F4, NOTE_F4,

NOTE_F4, NOTE_G4, NOTE_E4, NOTE_E4, NOTE_D4, NOTE_C4, NOTE_C4, NOTE_D4,

0, NOTE_A3, NOTE_C4, NOTE_B3, NOTE_D4, NOTE_B3, NOTE_E4, NOTE_F4,

NOTE_F4, NOTE_C4, NOTE_C4, NOTE_C4, NOTE_C4, NOTE_D4, NOTE_C4,

NOTE_D4, 0, 0, NOTE_A3, NOTE_C4, NOTE_D4, NOTE_D4, NOTE_D4, NOTE_F4,

NOTE_G4, NOTE_G4, NOTE_G4, NOTE_A4, NOTE_A4, NOTE_A4, NOTE_A4, NOTE_G4,

NOTE_A4, NOTE_D4, 0, NOTE_D4, NOTE_E3, NOTE_F4, NOTE_F4, NOTE_G4, NOTE_A4,

NOTE_D4, 0, NOTE_D4, NOTE_F4, NOTE_E4, NOTE_E4, NOTE_F4, NOTE_D4

```
};

int Pirates_duration[] = {

4,8,4,8,4,8,8,8,8,4,8,4,8,4,8,8,8,8,4,8,4,8,

4,8,8,8,8,4,4,8,8,4,4,8,8,4,4,8,8,

8,4,8,8,8,4,4,8,8,4,4,8,8,4,4,8,4,

4,8,8,8,8,4,4,8,8,4,4,8,8,4,4,8,8,

8,4,8,8,8,4,4,4,8,4,8,8,8,4,4,8,8

};

//###########End    of    He    is    a    Pirate
song#############//
```

The above square of code shows the note worth and note length of "He is a Pirate" subject structure the motion picture Pirates of the Caribbean. You can include your subject also like this.

Schematic and Hardware:

The schematic of this Arduino Tone Generator Project task is appeared in the figure underneath:

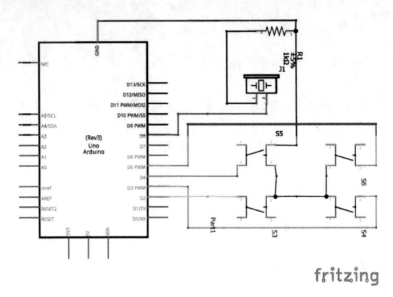

fritzing

The association is really straightforward we have a Piezo speaker which is associated with stick 8 and Ground of the Arduino through a 1K resistor. This 1k resistor is a present constraining resistor, which is utilized to keep the current inside as far as possible. We likewise have four changes to choose the necessary tune. One finish of the switch is associated with ground and the opposite end is associated with stick 2, 3, 4 and 5 individually. The switches will have draw up resistors empowered inside utilizing the product. Since the circuit is quite basic it tends to be interface utilizing a bread board as demonstrated as follows:

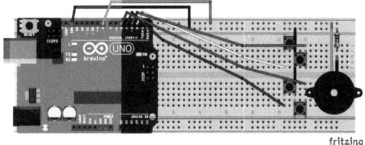

fritzing

Arduino Program Explanation:

When you have comprehended the idea, the Arduino program is really straight forward. The total code is given toward the finish of the instructional exercise. In the event that you are inexperienced with including header documents you can install the code as a ZIP record from here and legitimately transfer it to your Arduino.

The over two are the header records that must be included. "pitches.h" is utilized to liken every melodic note to a specific recurrence and "themes.h" contains the note worth and note term of all the four tones.

```
#include "pitches.h"

#include "themes.h"
```

A capacity is made to play each tone when required.

Here when the capacity Play_Pirates() is known as the "He is a Pirate" tone will be played. This capacity comprises of the tone work which creates the recurrence at stick number 8. The noTone(8) is called to stop the music once it's played. On the off chance that you have to play your own tone, change the Pirates_note and Pirates_duration to the new note and term esteems that you have spared in "themes.h" esteem

```
void Play_Pirates()

{

  for (int thisNote = 0; thisNote < (sizeof(Pirates_note)/sizeof(int)); thisNote++) {

    int noteDuration = 1000 / Pirates_duration[thisNote];//convert duration to time delay

    tone(8, Pirates_note[thisNote], noteDuration);

    int pauseBetweenNotes = noteDuration * 1.05; // Here 1.05 is tempo, increase to play it slower

    delay(pauseBetweenNotes);

    noTone(8);
```

```
        }

}
```

The stick 2, 3, 4 and 5 are utilized to choose the specific tone to be played. These pins are held high as a matter of course utilizing the inner draw up resistors by utilizing the above line of code. At the point when the catch is squeezed it is dismantled down to ground.

```
pinMode(2, INPUT_PULLUP);

pinMode(3, INPUT_PULLUP);

pinMode(4, INPUT_PULLUP);

pinMode(5, INPUT_PULLUP);
```

Underneath square of code is utilized to play the melody when a catch is squeezed. It peruses the computerized estimation of each catch and when it gets low (zero) it expect that the catch is squeezed and plays the separate tone by calling the necessary capacity.

```
if(digitalRead(2)==0)

{ Serial.println("Selected -> 'He is a Pirate' ");
```

```
Play_Pirates(); }

if(digitalRead(3)==0)

{ Serial.println("Selected -> 'Crazy Frog' ");  Play_
CrazyFrog(); }

if(digitalRead(4)==0)

{ Serial.println("Selected -> 'Mario UnderWorld' ");
Play_MarioUW(); }

if(digitalRead(5)==0)

{ Serial.println("Selected -> 'He is a Pirate' ");
Play_Pirates(); }
```

Working of this Melody Player Arduino Circuit:

When your Code and Hardware is prepared, basically consume the program into your Arduino and you ought to have the option to play the tone by just squeezing the catches.

Expectation you appreciated the venture and would utilize it in a portion of your undertaking or make another tone for your task.

Code

```
#include "pitches.h" //add Equivalent frequency for musical note
#include "themes.h" //add Note vale and duration
void Play_Pirates()
{
   for (int thisNote = 0; thisNote < (sizeof(Pirates_note)/sizeof(int)); thisNote++) {
   int noteDuration = 1000 / Pirates_duration[thisNote];//convert duration to time delay
   tone(8, Pirates_note[thisNote], noteDuration);
   int pauseBetweenNotes = noteDuration * 1.05; // Here 1.05 is tempo, increase to play it slower
   delay(pauseBetweenNotes);
```

```
  noTone(8); //stop music on pin 8
  }
}
void Play_CrazyFrog()
{
   for (int thisNote = 0; thisNote < (sizeof(Crazy-
Frog_note)/sizeof(int)); thisNote++) {
   int noteDuration = 1000 / CrazyFrog_duration[this-
Note]; //convert duration to time delay
   tone(8, CrazyFrog_note[thisNote], noteDuration);
    int pauseBetweenNotes = noteDuration * 1.30;//
Here 1.30 is tempo, decrease to play it faster
   delay(pauseBetweenNotes);
   noTone(8); //stop music on pin 8
   }
}
void Play_MarioUW()
{
   for (int thisNote = 0; thisNote < (sizeof(MarioU-
W_note)/sizeof(int)); thisNote++) {
   int noteDuration = 1000 / MarioUW_duration[this-
Note];//convert duration to time delay
   tone(8, MarioUW_note[thisNote], noteDuration);
   int pauseBetweenNotes = noteDuration * 1.80;
   delay(pauseBetweenNotes);
   noTone(8); //stop music on pin 8
   }
}
void Play_Titanic()
```

```
{
    for (int thisNote = 0; thisNote < (sizeof(Titanic_note)/sizeof(int)); thisNote++) {
    int noteDuration = 1000 / Titanic_duration[thisNote];//convert duration to time delay
   tone(8, Titanic_note[thisNote], noteDuration);
   int pauseBetweenNotes = noteDuration * 2.70;
   delay(pauseBetweenNotes);
   noTone(8); //stop music on pin 8
   }
}
void setup() {
pinMode(2, INPUT_PULLUP); //Button 1 with internal pull up
pinMode(3, INPUT_PULLUP); //Button 2 with internal pull up
pinMode(4, INPUT_PULLUP); //Button 3 with internal pull up
pinMode(5, INPUT_PULLUP); //Button 4 with internal pull up
Serial.begin(9600);
}
void loop() {
  if (digitalRead(2)==0)
      { Serial.println("Selected -> 'He is a Pirate' ");
 Play_Pirates(); }
  if (digitalRead(3)==0)
     { Serial.println("Selected -> 'Crazy Frog' ");  Play_
CrazyFrog(); }
  if (digitalRead(4)==0)
```

```
  { Serial.println("Selected -> 'Mario UnderWorld' ");
Play_MarioUW(); }
  if(digitalRead(5)==0)
    { Serial.println("Selected -> 'Titanic' ");  Play_Ti-
tanic(); }
}
```

10. STEP BY STEP INSTRUCTIONS TO SEND DATA TO WEB SERVER UTILIZING ARDUINO AS WELL AS SIM900A GPRS/ GSM MODULE

Here with an intriguing venture with regards to which we will Send Data to the SparkFun server utilizing Arduino and GPRS. This is an IoT based venture and we will utilize GPRS, present on the GSM Module

SIM900A board, to send a few information to the web administration on the web.

In this undertaking, we will essentially enter some content utilizing 4x4 Alphanumeric keypad and send it to SparkFun site utilizing Arduino and GPRS, from where you can see that information from anyplace in the word through web. Here we have additionally appended a 16x2 LCD to see the information locally. This information sending procedure is exceptionally valuable in IoT ventures where you need to screen things from anywhere on the planet like Monitoring Temperature and Humidity, Monitor Heart Beat , Monitor Vehicle Location, Monitor Air contamination level and so forth.

Components Required:

- Arduino
- 16x2 LCD
- GSM Module SIM900A
- Breadboard or PCB
- 4x4 Matrix Keypad
- Power supply 12v
- Connecting jumper wire
- SIM Card

Using GPRS in GSM Module:

Here we have utilized an ordinary GSM Module with a SIM card for GPRS association. In this venture, GPRS is liable for sending information to the Sparkfun server. Beforehand we have done numerous undertakings where we have utilized Wi-Fi module ESP8266 to send information to various servers over web. In any case, this time we have utilized GPRS.

GPRS is a parcel based remote correspondence administration that works with information pace of 56-114kbps and gives an association with the web.

For GPRS, we don't have to purchase any extraordinary module or equipment in light of the fact that GSM as of now has GPRS offices inbuilt. We just need to get to it by utilizing a similar strategy or AT directions that we utilized for GSM interfacing in our past undertakings. There are numerous AT directions previously referenced in the datasheet of SIMCOM SIM900A GSM module.

Presently for sending information to server by utilizing GPRS, first we have to instate GSM module.

Directions for instating GSM:

AT :- this command is used to check whether GSM module is responding or not.

AT+CPIN? :- this command is used to check whether SIM card is inserted in GSM Module or not.

ATE0 :- is used for disabling echo

ATE1 :- is used for enabling echo

Directions for instating GPRS web association:

AT+CIPSHUT :- to close TCP Port Explicitly means disconnect connection if any

AT+CGATT? :- Checking SIM card has internet connection or not

AT+CSTT = "APN","userName","Pass" :- connect to internet

(ex; AT+CSTT="airtelgprs.com","","")

AT+CIICR :- bring up with the wireless network. Checking SIM card has data pack or balance

AT+CIFSR :- get IP (sometimes without this command GSM do not work so use this command)

AT+CIPSTART = "TCP","SERVER IP","PORT" :- is used for creating TCP connection with the server that we provide in place of SERVER IP

AT+CIPSEND :- this command is used for sending data to the server. After input, this command server asks for data.

Subsequent to contributing the information we send 26 to the server. In case there is no reason to worry, at that point information will be presented effectively on the server and SparkFun server reacts with a pass or bomb string.

```
AT+CIPSTART="TCP","data.sparkfun.com",80

OK

CONNECT OK
AT+CIPSEND=90

> GET /input/w5nXxM6rpOtww5YVYg3G?private_key=wY9DPG5vzpH99KNrNkx2&log=SPARKFUN HTTP/1.0

SEND OK
HTTP/1.1 200 OK
Access-Control-Allow-Origin: *
Access-Control-Allow-Methods: GET,POST,DELETE
Access-Control-Allow-Headers: X-Requested-With, Phant-Private-Key
Content-Type: text/plain
X-Rate-Limit-Limit: 300
X-Rate-Limit-Remaining: 298
X-Rate-Limit-Reset: 1497469452.003
Date: Wed, 14 Jun 2017 19:31:22 GMT
Connection: close
Set-Cookie: SERVERID=; Expires=Thu, 01-Jan-1970 00:00:01 GMT; path=/
Cache-control: private

1 success

CLOSED
```

Working Explanation:

Procedure of Sending Data from GPRS of GSM Module is simple. Here in this venture, we are sending some string or words to the server by composing utilizing keypad. Same string or word will show up over the LCD, at that point press D/OK to send the info string to the server. Here we have made an Alphanumeric Keypad for contributing the characters or numeric qualities to Arduino or LCD. C/clear is customized for delete.

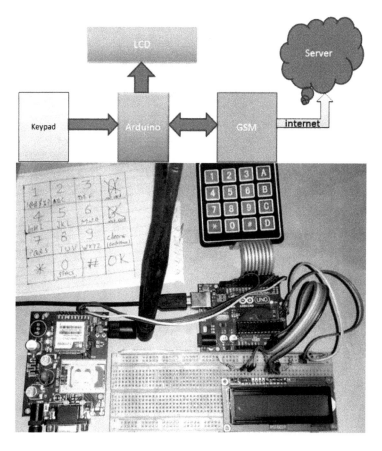

Alphanumeric is a technique to enter numbers and letters in order both by utilizing the equivalent 4x4 grid Kepad keypad. Here we have coded the equivalent 4x4 keypad for Arduino to acknowledge letters in order too. Check the full code toward the finish of the article.

Circuit Explanation:

For Sending Data to SparkFun Server, we have to interface Keypad as well as GSM module to Arduino. In this task we have utilized Arduino to taking information string from the keypad and sending directions to GSM/GPRS module. GSM/GPRS is utilized to speak with the Internet for sending information to the Sparkfun server. GSM Module's Rx and Tx stick is straightforwardly associated with Arduino's stick D3 and D2 separately (Ground of Arduino and GSM must be associated with one another). A 16x2 LCD is utilized for showing information strings and demonstrating welcome message and information sending status also. Pins of this 16x2 LCD to be specific Rs, en, d4, d5, d6, and d7 are associated with stick number 14, 15, 16, 17, 18 and 19 of Arduino separately. A 4x4 keypad is utilized for information string to Arduino and its Row pins R1, R2, R3, R4 are straightforwardly connected to stick number 11,10, 9, 8 of Arduino and Colum stick of keypad C1, C2, C3 are connected with stick number 7, 6, 5,4 of Arduino.

Here we have likewise associated GSM Tx stick to Tx of Arduino to get reaction information over the sequential screen.

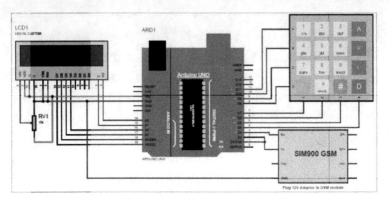

Programming Explanation:

Programming some portion of this venture is some-what perplexing for learners yet by doing a tad practice and focusing you can get it. In this code, we have utilized keypad library for interfacing straightforward keypad for entering numbers. Also, for entering letter sets we have utilized a similar library and keypad however utilized one more capacity to make it alphanumeric keypad. Means we have made each key multi-working and can enter every one of the characters and whole numbers by utilizing just 10 keys.

In the event that we press key 2 (ABC2), it will show 'An' and in case we press it once more, at that point it will supplant 'A' with 'B' and in the event that again we press it, at that point it will show 'C' at a similar spot in LCD. In case we sit tight for quite a while in the wake of squeezing a key, the cursor will consequently move to next position in LCD. Presently we can enter next burn or number. Furthermore, same technique is applied to different keys. It works same as keypad in old cell phones.

Underneath we have included Keypad.h library and characterize exhibit lattice for the keys:

```
#include <Keypad.h>          // keypad library for
interfacing keypad

const byte ROWS = 4; //four rows

const byte COLS = 4; //four columns

int x=0;

int y=0;

int n=0;

int minValue=0;

int maxValue=0;

char keyPress=0;

int keyPressTime=100;

String msg="";
```

```
char hexaKeys[ROWS][COLS] =

{

 {'1','2','3','A'},

 {'4','5','6','B'},

 {'7','8','9','C'},

 {'*','0','#','D'}

};

byte rowPins[ROWS] = {11, 10, 9, 8}; //connect to
the row pinouts of the keypad

byte colPins[COLS] = {7, 6, 5, 4}; //connect to the
column pinouts of the keypad
```

Also, given void get key capacity is utilized for input letters in order

```
void getkey(int minValue, int maxValue, char key-
Press)

{

  int ch=minValue;
```

```
int pressed=1;

char key=keyPress;

lcd.noBlink();

for(int i=0;i<keyPressTime;i++)

{

  if(key==keyPress)

  {

    lcd.setCursor(x,y);

    lcd.print(alpha[ch]);

    ch++;

    if(ch>maxValue)

    ch=minValue;

    i=0;

  }

  ....
```

.....

Underneath void initGSM() and void initGPRS() capacities are utilized for introducing GSM module and GPRS

```
void initGSM()

{

  connectGSM("AT","OK");

  connectGSM("ATE1","OK");

  connectGSM("AT+CPIN?","READY");

}

void initGPRS()

{

  connectGSM("AT+CIPSHUT","OK");

  connectGSM("AT+CGATT=1","OK");

  connectGSM("AT+CSTT=\"airtelgprs.com\",\"\",
\"\"","OK");
```

```
connectGSM("AT+CIICR","OK");

delay(1000);

Serial1.println("AT+CIFSR");

delay(1000);

}
```

Underneath some portion of the code is utilized to make URL and send the information to server by means of URL.

```
else if(key == 'D')

  {

    lcd.clear();

    lcd.noBlink();

    lcd.print("Sending Data");

    lcd.setCursor(0,1);

    lcd.print("To Server");

    url="GET /input/";
```

```
url+=publicKey;

url+="?private_key=";

url+=pvtKey;

url+="&log=";

url+=msg;

url+=" HTTP/1.0\r\n\r\n";

String svr=Start+","+ip+","+port;

delay(1000);

connectGSM(svr,"CONNECT");

delay(1000);

int len = url.length();

String str="";

str=SendCmd+len;

sendToServer(str);
```

So this is the means by which we can send any information, on the Spark Fun server through GPRS, to be checked from any place on the planet.

Code

```
#include <SoftwareSerial.h>   // serial software library for interfacing gsm module
SoftwareSerial Serial1(2, 3); // RX, TX // connect gsm Tx at D2 and Rx at D3

#include<LiquidCrystal.h>   // LCD library for interfacing LCD
LiquidCrystal lcd(14,15,16,17,18,19);   // connect rs,en,d4,d5,d6,d7 respectevely

String pvtKey="wY9DPG5vzpH99KNrNkx2";  // private key for posting data to sparkfun
String publicKey="w5nXxM6rp0tww5YVYg3G";  // public key for open page of sparkfun
String url="";
String ip="\"data.sparkfun.com\"";   // sparkfun server ip or url
int port=80;              // sparkfun server port
String SendCmd="AT+CIPSEND=";    // sending number of byte command
String Start="AT+CIPSTART=\"TCP\"";  // TCPIP start command
// strings and variables
//String msg="";
String instr="";
String str_sms="";
String str1="";
int i=0,temp=0;
```

```
#include <Keypad.h>          // keypad library for
interfacing keypad
const byte ROWS = 4; //four rows
const byte COLS = 4; //four columns
int x=0;
int y=0;
int n=0;
int minValue=0;
int maxValue=0;
char keyPress=0;
int keyPressTime=100;
String msg="";
char hexaKeys[ROWS][COLS] =
{
 {'1','2','3','A'},
 {'4','5','6','B'},
 {'7','8','9','C'},
 {'*','0','#','D'}
};
byte rowPins[ROWS] = {11, 10, 9, 8}; //connect to the
row pinouts of the keypad
byte colPins[COLS] = {7, 6, 5, 4}; //connect to the col-
umn pinouts of the keypad
Keypad              customKeypad              =
Keypad( makeKeymap(hexaKeys), rowPins, colPins,
ROWS, COLS);
String   alpha="1!@_$%?ABC2DEF3GHI4JKL5MNO-
6PQRS7TUV8WXYZ9*0#";
void setup()
{
```

```
Serial1.begin(9600);  // init serial1 for GSM
lcd.begin(16,2);    // init LCD
lcd.print("Sending Data ");
lcd.setCursor(0,1);
lcd.print("to Server");
delay(2000);
lcd.clear();
lcd.print("Hello world");
lcd.setCursor(0,1);
lcd.print("Saddam Khan");
delay(2000);
lcd.clear();
lcd.print("Initializing GSM");
initGSM();   // init GSM module
lcd.clear();
lcd.print("Initializing GPRS");
initGPRS();   // init GPRS in GSM Module
lcd.clear();
lcd.print("System Ready");
delay(2000);
}
void loop()
{
 int n=0;
 lcd.clear();
 lcd.noCursor();
 while(1)
 {
  lcd.cursor();
  char key = customKeypad.getKey();
```

```
if(key=='1')
 getkey(0, 6, key);
if(key=='2')
 getkey(7, 10, key);
else if(key=='3')
 getkey(11, 14, key);
else if(key=='4')
 getkey(15, 18, key);
else if(key=='5')
 getkey(19, 22, key);
else if(key=='6')
 getkey(23, 26, key);
else if(key=='7')
 getkey(27, 31, key);
else if(key=='8')
 getkey(32,35, key);
else if(key=='9')
 getkey(36, 40, key);
else if(key=='*')
 getkey(41, 41, key);
else if(key=='0')
 getkey(42, 43, key);
else if(key=='#')
 getkey(44, 44, key);

  else if(key == 'C')
{
   x--;
```

```
      lcd.setCursor(x,y);
      lcd.print(" ");
      n--;
      msg[n]=' ';
      lcd.setCursor(x,y);
   }
   else if(key == 'D')
   {
    lcd.clear();
    lcd.noBlink();
    lcd.print("Sending Data");
    lcd.setCursor(0,1);
    lcd.print("To Server");
    url="GET /input/";
    url+=publicKey;
    url+="?private_key=";
    url+=pvtKey;
    url+="&log=";
    url+=msg;
    url+=" HTTP/1.0\r\n\r\n";
    String svr=Start+","+ip+","+port;
    delay(1000);
    connectGSM(svr,"CONNECT");
    delay(1000);
    int len = url.length();
    String str="";
    str=SendCmd+len;
    sendToServer(str);
    Serial1.print(url);
    delay(1000);
```

```
 Serial1.write(0x1A);
 delay(1000);
 lcd.clear();
 lcd_status();
 // clearmsg();
 n=0;
 i=0;
 x=0;
 y=0;
 msg="";
 }
 }
}
void getkey(int minValue, int maxValue, char key-
Press)
{
 int ch=minValue;
 int pressed=1;
 char key=keyPress;
 lcd.noBlink();
 for(int i=0;i<keyPressTime;i++)
 {
  if(key==keyPress)
  {
   lcd.setCursor(x,y);
   lcd.print(alpha[ch]);
   ch++;
   if(ch>maxValue)
   ch=minValue;
   i=0;
```

```
   }
   key=customKeypad.getKey();
   delay(10);
  }
  if(pressed)
  {
   x++;
   msg+=alpha[ch-1];
   n++;
   if(x>15)
   {
    x=0;
    y=1;
   }
  }
  pressed=0;
  lcd.blink();
}
void lcd_status()
{
 lcd.clear();
 lcd.print("Data Sent to");
 lcd.setCursor(0,1);
 lcd.print("Server");
 delay(2000);
 lcd.clear();
}
void sendToServer(String str)
{
 Serial1.println(str);
```

```
 delay(1000);
}
void initGSM()
{
 connectGSM("AT","OK");
 connectGSM("ATE1","OK");
 connectGSM("AT+CPIN?","READY");
}
void initGPRS()
{
 connectGSM("AT+CIPSHUT","OK");
 connectGSM("AT+CGATT=1","OK");
     connectGSM("AT+CSTT=\"airtelgprs.com\",\"\",
\"\"","OK");
 connectGSM("AT+CIICR","OK");
 delay(1000);
 Serial1.println("AT+CIFSR");
 delay(1000);
}
void connectGSM (String cmd, char *res)
{
 while(1)
 {
  Serial.println(cmd);
  Serial1.println(cmd);
  delay(500);
  while(Serial1.available()>0)
  {
   if(Serial1.find(res))
   {
```

```
  delay(1000);
  return;
 }
}
 delay(1000);
 }
}
/*
```

Public URL

http://data.sparkfun.com/streams/
w5nXxM6rp0tww5YVYg3G

Public Key

w5nXxM6rp0tww5YVYg3G

Private Key

wY9DPG5vzpH99KNrNkx2

Keep this key secret, and in a safe place. You will not be able to retrieve it.

Delete Key

xxxxxxxxxxxxx

This key can only be used once. Keep this key secret, and in a safe place. You will not be able to retrieve it.

Logging using query string parameters
Format:

http://data.sparkfun.com/input/[publicKey]?
private_key=[privateKey]&log=[value]

Example:

http://data.sparkfun.com/input/
w5nXxM6rp0tww5YVYg3G?
private_key=wY9DPG5vzpH99KNrNkx2&
log=22.21

Anbazhagan K

*/

www.ingramcontent.com/pod-product-compliance
Lightning Source LLC
LaVergne TN
LVHW051226050326
832903LV00028B/2265

ISBN 9781703103892